TRAVELLING CRANE.

VIEW OF PORT SAID BREAKWATERS, SUEZ CANAL.

PORT SAID LIGHT HOUSE.

REPORT

ON THE

HYDRAULIC LIME OF TEIL,

TO

MESSRS. H. CHAMPIN AND GILLET,

SOLE REPRESENTATIVES AND AGENTS FOR NORTH AMERICA OF MM. L. & E. PAVIN DE LAFARGE AND SOULLIER & BRUNOT, THE ONLY MANUFACTURERS IN FRANCE,

9 NASSAU STREET, NEW YORK.

FABRICATION AND USE,

IN THE

CONSTRUCTION OF MARINE WORKS, CANALS, AQUEDUCTS, SEWERS, TUNNELS, RAILROADS, BRIDGES, BUILDINGS, FOUNDATIONS, FLOORS, ARTIFICIAL STONE, ETC., ETC.

BY

LEONARD F. BECKWITH,
CIVIL ENGINEER,
GRADUATE OF THE ECOLE CENTRALE DES ARTS ET MANUFACTURES, PARIS; MEMBER OF THE AMERICAN SOCIETY OF CIVIL ENGINEERS, CORRESPONDING MEMBER OF THE AMERICAN INSTITUTE OF ARCHITECTS.

NEW YORK:
D. VAN NOSTRAND, PUBLISHER,
23 MURRAY AND 27 WARREN STREET.
1873.

CONTENTS.

PAGE

Preface 7

Fabrication of Teil Hydraulic Lime:

- General Description 9
- Quarries 9
- Burning 10
- Slaking 10
- Screening 10
- Packing 11

Composition, Strength, and Methods of Using Teil Hydraulic Lime:

- Analyses of Teil Limestone 12
- Analyses of Teil Hydraulic Lime 13
- Theory of Concretion 13
- Weight of Teil Hydraulic Lime 16
- Tests of Strength 16
- Slaking and Mixing 18
- Proportions of Teil Mortars and Betons 19

Applications of Teil Hydraulic Lime:

- Marine Structures 21
- Investigations 21
- Action of Sea-Water on Mortars 22
- Comparison between Teil Lime and Cements 23
- Action of Sea-Water on Teil Lime 26
- Action of Salts of Magnesia 26
- Action of Carbonic Acid 28
- Plants and Shells 29
- Storms and Currents 29
- Tides 29
- Economy of Teil Lime compared with Cements 30
- Use of Teil Lime in Seaports 32

PAGE

APPLICATION OF TEIL HYDRAULIC LIME:
Marseilles 33
Toulon 34
Algiers 34
Port Said 34
Alexandria 35
General Observations 36
Canals, Sewers, Aqueducts 37
Bridges, Railroads, Tunnels 38
Warehouses, Buildings, Foundations, Cellars 38
Artificial Stones 39
Bricks and Slabs for Floors and Partition Walls 40

CONCLUSION 40

APPENDIX.

FABRICATION OF ARTIFICIAL BLOCKS OF TEIL BETON AT MARSEILLES:
General Description of the Yard of Fabrication 41
Fabrication of the Mortar. Proportions 43
Fabrication of the Beton and Blocks. Proportions 45
Lifting, Loading, and Transportation of the Blocks 49
Employment of Artificial Blocks 51
Jetties 51
Quay Walls 52
Personnel and Labor required 54
Description of a Smaller Yard of Fabrication 56
Cost of Fabrication of Teil Beton Blocks—Marseilles—New York. 57

CERTIFICATES:
Port of Marseilles 61
Port Said, Suez Canal 64
Port of Toulon 65
Port of Cette 66
Port Vendres 66
Port of St. Malo 67
Pointe de Grave 67
Port of St. Jean de Luz 68
Port of Barcelona 68
Port of Algiers 69
Port of Oran 70
Port of Philippeville 70

PAGE

CERTIFICATES:

Port of Ajaccio 71
Port of Bastia 71
Port of Isle-Rousse 73
Port of La Spezzia 73
City of Tunis 74
City of Odessa 75
Province of Constantine 75
Canal of Forez 76
Mt. Cenis Tunnel 76
Railroads 77

LIST OF PLATES.

FRONTISPIECE.—VIEW OF BREAKWATERS, SUEZ CANAL.

PLATE I.—GREAT JETTY AND QUAY WALLS OF ARTIFICIAL BLOCKS OF TEIL BETON, PORT NAPOLEON, MARSEILLES.

II.—GENERAL PLAN OF LA JOLIETTE YARD OF FABRICATION OF TEIL BETON BLOCKS, MARSEILLES.

III.—CROSS-SECTION OF MORTAR MILL BUILDING.

IV.—PLAN OF FLOOR OF STEAM MORTAR MILLS.

V.—SAND CAR. ELEVATION, PLAN, AND SECTION.

VI.—PEBBLE CAR. " " "

VII.—MORTAR CAR. " " "

VIII.—MIXING CYLINDER FOR BETON. ELEVATIONS, PLAN, AND SECTION.

PREFACE.

At the request of Messrs. H. Champin and Gillet, I have prepared, upon the Hydraulic Lime of Teil, the following observations, which are drawn from numerous reports upon the subject, from private sources, and from a personal knowledge of the value and applications of this lime.

LEONARD F. BECKWITH, C. E.

111 Broadway,
New York, *February*, 1873.

REPORT

ON THE

HYDRAULIC LIME OF TEIL.

FABRICATION OF TEIL HYDRAULIC LIME.

GENERAL DESCRIPTION.

Quarries.—The limestone quarries of Teil are situated on the banks of the River Rhone (Canton of Viviers, Department of Ardeche, France), and have been worked for several centuries. They produce a silicious hydraulic lime celebrated for its capacity to resist the destructive action of the sea. It is known in commerce under the name of *Hydraulic Lime of Teil.*

The quarries of Teil belong to the Lower Neocomian Marls of the Cretaceous Formation, and constitute the beds known to geologists under the name of *criocera limestones*, so-called from the resemblance of their fossil shells to a "ram's horn." These beds are worked by two companies, Messrs. Pavin de Lafarge, and Messrs. Soullier & Brunot. As the method of fabrication is the same in both companies a description of the works of the first will suffice.

The Lafarge quarries are opened on a length of 1,470 feet with an average height of 400 feet, and consist of three superposed layers of compact and homogeneous stone. The limestone is chiefly mined by the help of acid, which eats a cavity at the bottom of the drill hole and enables a heavier blast to be obtained.

The quantity of broken stone daily burnt averages 818 cubic yards, corresponding to a product of 500 tons of screened lime.

Burning.—The works, situated on the river bank at the foot of the quarries, contain 34 continuous lime kilns, which consume daily 100 tons of coal. Each kiln has a daily capacity of 130 cubic yards of lime. The heat at which the limestone is burnt is only sufficient to expel the carbonic acid and not to vitrify any part of the stone. The doors of the kilns open into vast sheds where the burnt lime goes through the process of slaking.

Slaking.—The slaking of hydraulic limes is always attended with difficulty, owing to the presence of lumps of burnt stone harder than the rest, and which cannot be slaked without previous crushing. These portions make a mortar of irregular consistency, and by slaking subsequently in the masonry might destroy it; moreover, danger attends the transportation of unslaked lime.

The above considerations have caused the general adoption of slaking hydraulic limes at the works. Formerly the slaking was done with a copious use of water; this practice has been discontinued, and slaking by sprinkling substituted. The burnt lime direct from the kilns, in thin layers, is lightly sprinkled with water, by a workman with a hose. The sprinkled lime falls into powder, is shovelled into heaps, and the slaking is completed by the help of the steam evolved, which penetrates the interstices of the mass. The lime remains in heaps about ten days; at the end of this time it is in sufficiently fine powder to be screened.

Screening.—The screens, similar to those used in flour mills, consist of sieves of No. 40 fine wire cloth, of 50 brass wires to a lineal inch. In the burning of lime, portions of the stone are imperfectly calcined; this arises either from the fire not reaching them, or from their peculiar chemical composition being unfavorable to burning at the low temperature employed. These unburnt portions are separated by a coarse sieve placed over the hopper of the shute leading to each screen. The burnt lime fully slaked in powder passes through the coarse sieve into each screen, from which it falls into a collecting chamber below. The bottom of this chamber, or flour-bin, consists of hoppers by which the lime is drawn off for packing.

The fine lime in powder, passing through the screen, leaves behind it numerous particles of the size of grains of sand. These particles are calcareous concretions, which do not contain sufficient free lime to become reduced to powder by slaking; they form in reality a natural cement which is a valuable addition to the hydraulic energy of the lime. The screenings are therefore collected and ground to powder, this operation being substituted for slaking, which was found to be impossible. A small elevator of sheet iron buckets on an endless chain returns the ground screenings to the screens, where their admixture with the slaked lime in powder coming from the kilns takes place uniformly and regularly. The grinding of the screenings keeps 19 pairs of grindstones constantly at work.

This method of slaking and screening Teil hydraulic lime at the works before delivery, has been practised since 1845. It is from this date that the use of Teil lime in powder spread rapidly throughout France.

Packing.--Teil hydraulic lime, slaked and screened ready for delivery, is a fine impalpable powder, and very homogeneous. It is usually packed in linen sacks of uniform size, which contain 110¼ pounds (50 kilogrammes) net weight of lime in powder. Uniformity in weight is obtained by a simple apparatus consisting of a suspended Beam Scales; the short arm holds the sack under the mouth of the hopper until, the weight of 110¼ pounds being reached, the beam descends; the packer closes the slide of the hopper, delivers the sack to be closed and sealed, and places another sack in its place. The sacks are closed and sealed with lead at the works, and the buyer is secured against fraud.

Packed in this way, Teil hydraulic lime has been shipped to a great distance by railroad and by sea, without suffering deterioration. For long voyages, however, a new method of packing it in barrels of 468 pounds net weight has been adopted. The barrels contain a lining or bag of thick gummed brown paper hermetically sealed, which preserves the lime during any length of time from alteration through absorption of carbonic acid and water from the air. Thick brown paper is an excellent non-conductor, and is air-tight.

Teil hydraulic lime is less liable than cements to alteration, as it depends chiefly for its hydraulic energy on silicate of lime, which after hydration contains 27 per cent. of its own weight of water.

One hundred pounds of Teil lime contain about 66 pounds of silicate of lime, which require 25.7 pounds of water for hydration; Teil lime in powder may thus absorb small quantities of water without much danger of alteration.

The establishment of Messrs. Pavin de Lafarge contains besides the 34 lime-kilns, 30 screens, 19 pairs of grindstones, 4 steam-engines, 1 water-wheel, and is well supplied with appliances such as tracks, docks, cranes and scales for handling lime. It employs 600 workmen and manufactures its own fire-brick, 2,000 tons annually, for the lime-kilns. The average yearly production is 100,000 tons of screened lime in powder. The size and completeness of these works enable the hydraulic lime to be manufactured on an extensive scale, and the product turned out is homogeneous and very uniform in composition.

COMPOSITION, STRENGTH, AND METHODS OF USING TEIL HYDRAULIC LIME.

Analyses.—Raw Teil Limestone analyzed by Professor Rivot, School of Mines, Paris, presents the following composition:

Lime	46.3
Oxide of Iron	0.7
Silica, Quartz Sand, and Clay	15.0
Carbonic Acid and Water	37.6

Teil limestone when dissolved in acid leaves an insoluble residue, varying from 12 to 17 per cent. of the total weight, and composed of free silica and quartz sand, with a very small quantity of clay. When analyzed this residue gives a constant proportion of 10 of silica to 1 of alumina; the clay, however, in its natural state is not attacked by chlorhydric acid.

The above analysis reveals the fact that a part of the silica is uncombined; though pulverulent, it is not easily dissolved by alkalies, as when Teil limestone is boiled with a diluted solution of $\frac{1}{10}$ of potash, only 1.87 per cent. of silica is dissolved; when the limestone is attacked by an acid, the silica remains as a muddy residue.

These characteristics indicate that Teil limestone belongs to the class of silicious hydraulic limestones.

After burning, Teil lime analysed by Professor Rivot gives the following composition:

Lime	78.29		73.60	
Oxide of Iron	traces		traces	
Silica	18.20	21.71	17.20	20.50
Alumina	1.80		1.70	
Quartz Sand	1.71		1.60	
Water and traces of Carbonic Acid	—		5.00	
	99.60		99.10	

Vicat gives the following analyses of Teil lime, containing a very small quantity of magnesia:

Lime	68.941		77.760	
Magnesia	0.612		0.541	
Silica	26.069	30.447	20.573	21.699
Alumina	4.378		1.126	
Peroxide of Iron	traces		traces	

The analyses show that Teil lime is very silicious and slow setting; it may be considered as the type of this variety of hydraulic limes, of which the mortars are remarkably durable in marine structures.

Theory of Concretion.—Silicious limes, like Teil hydraulic lime contain before burning, carbonate of lime, silica in fine sand, with a very small proportion of clay and oxide of iron.

By calcination at a low heat the carbonic acid is driven off, leaving an excess of quick-lime, with part of which the silica and alumina combine as silicate and aluminate of lime. The result is very uniformly:

70 to 80 per cent. of quick-lime;

30 to 20 per cent. of silicate of lime, with a small quantity of aluminate of lime, and uncombined quartz, intimately mixed.

$$CaO + Si\,O_3\,.\,3\,Ca\,O + Al_2\,O_3\,.\,3\,Ca\,O.$$

If the small quantity of alumina and iron is neglected, the composition of 100 lbs. of freshly burnt Teil lime is:

Silica	23
Lime	77

The 23 lbs. of silica are combined with 43 lbs. of lime, forming silicate of lime $SiO_3.\,3\,CaO$

{ Silica	23
{ Combined lime	43
Free or quick-lime	34

When slaked by sprinkling, the quick-lime alone is hydrated, the silicates and aluminates remain anhydrous (Chatoney and Rivot). Practice shows that 14 lbs. of water are required to slake 100 lbs. of fresh Teil lime; in consequence of evaporation, only 10 to 11 lbs. of water remain, which is the requisite quantity for hydrating 34 lbs. of free lime.

The hydraulic energy of the lime is due to the anhydrous condition of the silicate and aluminate of lime, which, when the mortar is subsequently mixed, form hydrosilicates and hydroaluminates of lime by combining with 6 equivalents of water, and crystallize.

$$Ca\,O.HO. + Si\,O_3.3\,Ca\,O.6\,HO. + Al_2\,O_3.3\,Ca\,O.6\,HO.$$

A perfect setting of mortar is due to the *simultaneous* crystallization of the above elements, which grasps and binds the grains of sand and gives strength and hardness to the mortar.

The dampness which mortars throw off in setting, is due to the crystallization, which, in taking place, absorbs only the necessary number of equivalents of water, and rejects the surplus; the energy of setting is in proportion to the absence of an excess of water.

The hardness of the interior of a mortar is due to the hardness of the crystals and to the slowness of their formation. It is increased by the subsequent evaporation of the excess of water, and the absorption by the lime of carbonic acid from the air, producing an enveloping crust of carbonate of lime. This absorption, which slowly progresses from the exterior inwards, requires considerable time in which to act.

An imperfect setting is due to the presence in the mortar of substances which do not crystallize simultaneously, but irregularly, some later than others. Sulphates of lime and magnesia crystallize more slowly than the elements above mentioned, and are very destructive to mortars, as, by expanding at the moment of crystallization, they produce cracks and fissures.

Silicate and aluminate of magnesia crystallize slower than the same combinations of lime, and their presence in moderate proportions is injurious, and produces disintegration or inferior hardness in parts of the mass after the general setting has occurred. (Rivot.) In considerable proportions, however, as in Rosendale cements, it is probable that the silicate and aluminate of magnesia cause the entire mass to partake of the character of their slower crystallization, and their presence is not injurious. Both silicate and aluminate of magnesia are strongly hydraulic, and when alone they resist very successfully the action of sea water; their value, however, in sea mortars in combination with silicate and aluminate of lime is questionable.

Unslaked particles of lime, which crystallize as hydrate of lime, subsequent to the setting of the mortar will swell and crack the mass. Sand and oxide of iron in lime act usually as inert substances.

A slow-setting hydraulic lime, such as Teil lime, crystallizes slowly, and produces well-defined and strong crystals; the slowness of setting is an additional guarantee against the disruption of mortar by the later crystallization of some of the elements. Quick-setting cements form a rapid and irregular crystallization of small crystals, and are, therefore, to be used with caution, where works of importance are undertaken.

To obtain a good mortar which will harden rapidly, it is essential to have the lime completely slaked, and to use only the quantity of water absolutely necessary to accomplish this in mixing. The latter should be very thorough, each particle of sand being coated with a thin envelope of lime.

An excess of either water or lime in proportion to sand is bad; the first makes a porous and friable mortar, and the second produces shrinkage, with loss of cohesion.

Weight of Teil Hydraulic Lime.—Teil hydraulic lime, slaked and screened, in powder, weighs per cubic foot, loose measure, 43¾ to 45 pounds. M. Noel, Director of the Arsenal Hydraulic Works, Toulon, gives as the weight of Teil lime, in powder, loose measure, 42½ to 43¾ lbs. per cubic foot. The weight per struck U. S. bushel, loose measure, is 54¼ to 56 pounds.

Tests of Strength.—The proportion of sand to lime has great influence upon the crushing and tensile strength of mortars. Numerous experiments with Teil mortars have been made by M. Pascal, Chief Engineer of the Works of the Port of Marseilles, and also by M. Noel, Director of the Hydraulic Works of the Naval Arsenal, Toulon (during the construction of three large graving docks, in which about 20,000 tons of Teil lime were employed, 1853 to 1865). The following tables are a summary of the tensile strength and crushing weight in pounds, per square inch, obtained in the above experiments with Teil mortars, after immersion in the sea during various lengths of time.

TABLE I.—(*Experiments of MM. Pascal and Noel.*)

TIME OF IMMERSION.	TENSILE STRENGTH IN POUNDS PER SQUARE INCH.				CRUSHING WEIGHT IN POUNDS PER SQUARE INCH.		
After 45 days	31.71	40.38	30.79	30.83	219.59	191.75	194.09
" 90 "	85.06	88.49	83.78	77.68	359.62	362.41	355.20
" 180 "	97.11	106.22	89.16	86.88	593.98	467.13	451.34
" 1 year	123.43	111.63	126.42	122.15	612.91	591.84	561.87
" 2 years	141.06	164.20	......	......	613.88	577.33	573.92

TABLE II.—(*Experiments of M. Pascal.*)

Mortar of 3 parts of Teil lime to 5 of sand, in volume.

TIME OF IMMERSION.	TENSILE STRENGTH IN POUNDS PER SQUARE INCH.	TIME OF IMMERSION.	CRUSHING WEIGHT IN POUNDS PER SQUARE INCH.
After 3 months....	57.59	After 15 days	121.70
" 6 "	86.03	" 30 "	184.29
" 22 "	121.30	" 45 "	266.77

TABLE III.

Mortar composed of 564½ pounds of Teil lime per cubic yard of sand containing 33% of voids.

AGE OF MORTAR.	TENSILE STRENGTH IN POUNDS PER SQUARE INCH.	AGE OF MORTAR.	CRUSHING WEIGHT IN POUNDS PER SQUARE INCH.
45 days........	38.42	45 days	205.04
90 "	83.77	90 "	259.15
180 "	94.86	180 "	504.24
1 year	120.94	1 year	588.99

In one instance a mortar composed of Teil lime and basaltic sand, after eight months immersion in the sea, acquired a tensile strength of 129.40 lbs. per square inch.

According to investigations made during the construction of the great Cherbourg Breakwater, the cohesive strength required in a mortar to withstand the battering action of the waves, should be about 29,500 lbs. per square yard, or 22¾ lbs. per square inch. The tables show conclusively that the mortars made with Teil lime have a greater strength than is required for masonry the most exposed to the sea.

Slaking and Mixing.—Teil lime unslaked, in lumps, weighs 36¼ lbs. per cubic foot. When slaked to a paste, the increase in volume is 0.35, and the increase in weight is 0.95.

Slaked and screened Teil lime in powder weighing $40\frac{3}{4}$ lbs. per cubic foot, made into paste, contracts in volume 0.41, with an increase in weight of 0.34.

The slaking of Teil quick-lime requires 14 lbs. of water per 100 lbs. of lime; subsequent evaporation leaves about 10 lbs., sometimes 7 lbs. of water remaining in one hundred of lime.

The hydration of 100 lbs. of Teil lime requires 28 lbs. of water; $1\frac{6}{10}$ cubic feet of lime paste containing 100 lbs. in powder will weigh, after taking, 128 lbs.

The taking of pure Teil hydraulic lime mortar occurs within 24 hours. After 18 hours the mortar sets strongly and will support the small Vicat needle, and in 24 hours the large needle. At the end of 48 hours it will support the Vicat drill with its full weight of $2\frac{1}{5}$ lbs. After the mortar has been immersed for 45 days in water 20 revolutions of the Vicat drill will penetrate to a depth of 0.0197 of an inch.

Hydraulic limes, in general, set too rapidly for the mortar paste to be prepared much in advance. Teil lime hardens rapidly, and if required to be used in paste, the mortar necessary for the day's work alone should be prepared. A preferable method is to mix the lime and sand dry in the desired proportions, and turn this dry mortar into paste as required. This method gives a more compact mortar with less water.

In mixing mortars, the importance of using as little water as possible, and making a perfect mixture by mechanical means, cannot be overestimated. In mixing Teil mortar salt and fresh water serve equally well.

When used for coating masonry, Teil hydraulic lime, like Portland cement, may be mixed the previous day, and re-mixed with additional water at the time of using it.

Proportions.—For one cubic yard of firm lime paste, 1,685 lbs. of Teil lime in powder are required, equivalent to 30 struck U. S. bushels, loose measure, of 56 lbs. per bushel. The proportion of lime per cubic yard of sand is regulated by the condition, that in good mortar the lime should fill the voids in the sand. The voids in loose damp sand vary from 0.31 to 0.35, and in compacted sand from 0.18 to 0.23 of the volume of sand.

With beton, the voids in the broken stone or pebbles vary from 0.35 to 0.40 of the volume, and the mortar should fill the voids.

For strictly impervious sea mortars made of fine and crumbling sands, in which the solidity depends solely upon the strength of the mortar, it is best to increase the proportion of Teil lime per cubic yard of sand to 10½ bushels, instead of 9 bushels, the usual quantity. With silicious or basaltic sands of average size this increase is unnecessary.

In fresh water the proportion of Teil lime has been successfully reduced to 253 lbs. per cubic yard of beton by Mr. Desplaces, Chief-Engineer of the Paris-Lyons-Mediterranean R. R. The best proportions for Teil *mortars* for various uses are the following ones, which fulfil the conditions previously mentioned. (The struck U. S. bushel of Teil lime in powder, loose measure, is taken at 56 lbs.)

For Mortars in Salt Water: (Beton under water.) 10½ U. S. bushels of Teil lime (590 lbs.) per cubic yard of sand, equivalent to 1 scant measure of lime to 2 full measures of sand.

For Mortars in Fresh Water: 9 U. S. bushels of Teil lime (506 lbs.) per cubic yard of sand, equivalent to 1¼ measures of lime to 3 measures of sand, making 1$\frac{1}{10}$ cubic yards of stiff mortar paste.

For Mortars exposed to Air: 7½ U. S. bushels of Teil lime (421 lbs.) per cubic yard of sand, equivalent to 1 measure of lime to 3 measures of sand.

For **Betons** the usual proportions of mortar and broken stone are:

In salt water 2	measures of mortar	to 3	of broken stone.	
In fresh water...................1	do.	do.	2	do.
Artificial blocks 1	do.	do.	2 of pebbles.	

The above proportions for Teil mortars and betons are adopted by the French Engineers of Bridges and Highways and by the Engineers of the Railroad Companies, in their specifications and contracts. The proportions are sanctioned by successful practice, and although it may be found best to vary them in different localities of the United States, according to the sand and water used, and other circumstances, the variations will probably be slight. These proportions show the advantages attending the use of Teil lime, which produces a strong mortar with a smaller weight of lime, than that of Portland Cement, generally employed for the same purposes. Teil hydraulic lime does not require special workmen, and unpractised laborers cannot fail to make good work with it.

APPLICATIONS OF TEIL HYDRAULIC LIME.

MARINE STRUCTURES.

Investigations.—The causes of the destruction of mortars by sea water have been made the subject of investigation in different countries. The length of time required before the results of experiments extending over a number of years could be obtained, has rendered progress slow. By the aid of analysis chemistry has ascertained the elements of limes and mortars, and the changes which they undergo in the various stages of manufacture and use. The comparison of these results with those obtained by the analysis of mortars which have withstood for years the destructive action of sea-water, has elicited a few general laws which govern the formation of hydraulic mortars, and which have removed to a great extent the obscurity which enveloped the subject. It is to Vicat and later to Berthier, Chatoney and Rivot, that the success of these investigations, and the important results which have followed them, are chiefly due.

Action of Sea-water on Mortars.—The action of salt water on mortars immersed in the sea, may briefly be stated as follows.

Sea water, constantly washing against mortar and renewing the surfaces in contact, slowly dissolves the hydrate of lime which has not had time to become carbonated. As this action continues, the hydrate of lime disappears, and by leaving the mortar porous, hastens the action of the salt water on the other elements. The aluminate and silicate of lime, remaining in contact with water holding in solution chloride of sodium (common salt), salts of magnesia, and carbonic acid, become decomposed in turn.

The aluminate of lime is first decomposed, forming aluminate of magnesia and lime, both of which disappear. The carbonic acid in the sea water then attacks the lime of the silicate of lime, producing carbonate of lime, which, as fast as it forms, is dissolved in the excess of water surrounding it. The silica alone remains in a pasty state, and the mortar crumbles away.

When, on the contrary, the mortar has had time to become carbonated by the free hydrate of lime absorbing carbonic acid from the air and water, and forming an impervious protecting shield to the mass, and when hydraulic limes derived from silicious limestones are employed instead of limes from argillaceous (aluminous) limestones, then the mortar will not be destroyed. The aluminates, which are the first elements to become decomposed, either do not exist at all in silicious limes, or else in very small quantities. The mortar no longer rendered porous will resist the action of the sea.

Vicat, Chatoney, and Rivot concluded from their investigations that the chief element of hydraulic energy in a lime is the presence of silicate of lime. The presence of alumina in limes and cements hastens the setting, but is no guarantee of durability, as it forms combinations with lime, which, as mentioned above, do not resist as well as silicates the action of salt water.

A careful examination of the mortars which have most successfully resisted the destructive action of the sea, disclosed the fact that they contained hydrosilicate of lime to the extent of 25 per cent. of the volume of the mortar. The greater the proportion of this element in a mortar, the greater will be its durability.

Teil hydraulic lime is a silicious lime, containing 66 per cent. of silicate of lime, a very small proportion of alumina, and a sufficient quantity of uncombined lime to form the protecting envelope of carbonate of lime, which is an important element for the preservation of mortars. Teil lime fulfils the requirements mentioned previously as necessary in sea-mortars.

It was first employed in marine structures in 1832, since which time its use has steadily increased. Teil lime formed one of the starting points in the investigations of Vicat, Chatoney, and Rivot, and the results stated in their reports justify their high opinion of its value for sea-mortars.

Comparison between Teil Lime and Cements.—A comparative examination of the elements of Teil hydraulic lime and of slow and quick-setting cements will be found interesting.

Table IV. gives the composition, by weight, of the elements of hydraulic energy in limes and cements:

TABLE IV.

Silicate of lime	$SiO_3 . 3\,CaO$.	Silica	23
		Lime	43
Silicate of alumina	$2\,SiO_3 . Al_2O_3$.	Silica	30
		Alumina	17
Aluminate of lime	$Al_2O_3 . 3\,CaO$.	Alumina	17
		Lime	28
Double silicate of lime and alumina	$SiO_3.(Al_2\,O_3 + CaO)_3$	Silica	15
		Alumina	51
		Lime	28
Silicate of magnesia	$SiO_3 . 3\,MgO$.	Silica	23
		Magnesia	30

The method of manufacture strongly influences the composition of limes and cements. At a high temperature, silicate of lime and the double silicate of lime and alumina are formed. At a low heat, the double silicate is not formed, and the alumina, acting towards the lime the part of an acid, produces aluminate of lime. By the first method, slow-setting cements, such as English, and Boulogne

Portland cements are manufactured; by the second method quick-setting cements, such as Vassy, etc., are produced.

On these facts as a basis, Table V. has been deduced in round numbers from the analyses of various cements, and is extracted from a Notice on the Hydraulic Lime of Teil, published in 1872.

Boulogne Portland cement may serve as an example of the method by which the table has been constructed. The analysis of this cement by Delesse, gives in one thousand parts:

Lime	651
Silica	204
Alumina	138
Magnesia	5.8

The fabrication is made at a high temperature; the double silicate of lime and alumina is first formed; 138 parts of alumina take up 40.24 parts of silica, the whole combining with 75 of lime, and forming 253.24 of double silicate of lime and alumina. There remain 163.76 of silica and 576 of lime. In the simple silicate of lime which is next formed, 163.76 of silica takes up 304 of lime, producing 467.67 of simple silicate of lime. Neglecting the small proportion of magnesia (5.8 parts in 1,000), there remain 273 parts of uncombined lime.

The composition of Boulogne Portland cement is then:

253 parts double silicate of lime and alumina.
467 parts simple silicate of lime.
273 parts free uncombined lime.

A similar calculation has been made in each instance.

TABLE V.

CEMENTS.	Double Silicate of Lime and Alumina.	Simple Silicate of Lime.	Aluminate of Lime.	Free Lime.	Free Silica.	Silicate of Magnesia.	Plaster (Sulphate of Lime).	REMARKS.
English Portland.	238	506	0	295	0	0	0	Resist the action of sea-water (English Portland to St. Malo). Slow-setting cements obtained at a very high heat (English Portland to Fagnerès).
Boulogne Portland	253	467	0	273	0	0	0	
Boulogne Ordinary	169	606	0	58	0	0	0	
Vitry (burnt)	201	540	0	198	0	0	0	
St. Malo.........	123	680	0	0	0	0	0	
Moissac..........	367	528	0	0	40	332	21	Do not resist the action of sea-water (Moissac to Fagnerès).
Porte de France ..	360	493	0	129	0	0	33	
Antony	146	791	0	0	18	0	40	
Fagnerès.........	273	450	0	0	263	0	12	
Vassy............	0	545	349	6	0	37	0	None of these cements resist the action of sea-water. Quick-setting cements obtained at an ordinary heat. (Vassy to La Valentine)
Porte de France ..	0	415	470	0	65	0	33	
Grenoble....	0	415	470	9	65	0	33	
Champ Rond.....	0	430	450	0	114	0	0	
Corbigny	0	488	370	0	75	0	44	
Vitry	0	634	291	26	0	0	0	
Gap	0	513	314	0	168	9	30	
La Valentine	0	545	349	6	0	37	0	
Teil hyd. lime ...	0	660	0	250	0	0	0	Resists sea-water.

A reference to the Table shows the large proportion of silicate of lime contained in Teil hydraulic lime, and explains the durability of Teil mortars, and their constantly increasing use. Teil lime is richer in silicate of lime than Portland or any cements of the Table. The proportions of aluminate of lime and silicate of magnesia in Teil lime are so small that they have been left out of the Table.

Action of Sea-water on Teil lime.—The action of sea-water on mortars varies in different seas, owing to variation in the proportions of destructive salts and gases contained in the sea. It is important to examine how Teil hydraulic lime in different localities, has stood the test of this action, and particularly that of salts of magnesia and carbonic acid.

Action of Salts of Magnesia.—Salts of magnesia are generally admitted to be the most destructive cause of decomposition in sea-mortars, although Rivot considers their action to be much exaggerated. Vicat in his experiments on hydraulic limes and cements employed a bath of sulphate of magnesia to test their durability. Table VI., by Vicat, gives the analysis of sea-water at different points.

TABLE VI.—(*Vicat.*)

SUBSTANCES CONTAINED IN 1000 PARTS OF WATER IN WEIGHT.	NEAR BAYONNE (ATLANTIC)	MEDITERRANEAN SEA.		NORTH ATLANTIC.	BRITISH CHANNEL.
Hydrochlorate of soda......	25.10	25.10	27.22	26.60	27.06
Sulphate of magnesia.......	5.78	6.25	7.02	"	2.29
Hydrochlorate of magnesia..	3.50	5.25	6.14	5.15	3.66
Sulphate of lime..........	0.15	0.15	0.10	0.15	1.41
Sulphate of soda..........	"	"	"	4.66	"
Hydrochlorate of potash....	"	"	0.01	1.23	0.76
Hydrochlorate of lime......	"	"	"	"	"
Carbonate of lime.........	0.20	0.15	0.20	"	0.03
Carbonic acid.............	0.23	0.11	Traces	"	Traces

TABLE VII.—(*Prof. Wolcott Gibbs.*)

(All sp. gr. refer to that of pure water at temperature of 14°C.)

LOCALITY.	DISTANCE BELOW SURFACE.	SPECIFIC GRAVITY.	SP. GR. AT TEMP. OF	SALINE MATTER PER CENT.	TEMP. F.	
					WATER.	AIR.
Washington Heights, H.R..	5′	1.0126	15°.25 C.	1.702	..	..
do.	6″	1.0111	15°.5 C.	1.585	30°	31°
Pier 1, Hudson River.	1′	1.0182	15°.2 C.	2.348	34½	36½
do.	5′	1.0192	18° C.	2.533	..	..
do.	1′	1.0183	15° C.	2.351	..	..
East River, foot 17th St....	5′	1.0185	16° C.	2.461	31	31½
do.	1′	1.0178	14° C.	2.463	31	31½
Buttermilk Channel	5′	1.0155	16° C.	2.132	35	41½
Vanderbilt Landing, S. I...	5′	1.0188	10° C.	2.533	..	..
do.	1′	1.0205	15°.5 C.	2.706	33	39½
Mouth Navesink River, N.J.	5′	1.0177	15° C.	2.513	33	33

Table VI. shows that the proportion of salts of magnesia is considerably greater in the Mediterranean than in the Atlantic Ocean and English Channel. As Teil hydraulic lime has been successfully employed in the Mediterranean for upwards of 40 years in marine structures, it is a fair inference to conclude that in the Atlantic Ocean this lime would give even better results, being exposed to a smaller proportion of magnesian salts. The artificial blocks made with Teil hydraulic lime at Cherbourg, the works at St. Malo, built upwards of fifteen years ago, and the large quay walls and docks of Bordeaux, which are being constructed with Teil lime, prove that in practice it resists equally well the action of the waters of the ocean and of the Mediterranean.

Table VII. derived from the U. S. Coast Survey Reports (1856), gives analyses of sea-water in the Harbor of New York. It shows that the proportion of saline matter is very similar on both sides of the Atlantic Ocean, and it is safe to presume that Teil lime will stand the test equally well here. A warm temperature of sea-water, such as exists in the Mediterranean, though favorable to the use of hydraulic mortars and beton at the time of formation, is unfavorable subsequently, and tends to facilitate decomposition in the sea.

Action of Carbonic Acid.—With regard to the action of carbonic acid on sea mortars, it is maintained by Vicat, Chatoney, and Rivot, that its presence in sea-water in a certain proportion is beneficial for the preservation of mortars, a crust of carbonate of lime being formed. This envelope is essential for the preservation of a mortar, and hydraulic limes and cements which do not contain free lime capable of absorbing carbonic acid, and thus forming carbonate of lime, should be used with caution. An excess, however, of carbonic acid in sea-water is a disadvantage. As was mentioned previously in treating of the action of sea-water on mortars, lime has a stronger affinity for carbonic acid than it has either for silica or alumina. The decomposition of the silicate, and particularly of the aluminate of lime is to be feared in waters highly charged with carbonic acid, and hydraulic limes and cements containing alumina in considerable quantity are in greater danger of destruction from this cause than silicious limes, such as Teil hydraulic lime.

The proportion of carbonic acid in the Mediterranean is variable; abundant in some localities, entirely deficient in others. Admitting that wherever Teil hydraulic lime has been employed in that sea, carbonic acid exists in considerable quantities, it is easy to ascertain the amount absorbed.

Chatoney and Rivot analyzed numerous samples of Teil hydraulic lime from blocks immersed in the sea at Marseilles. The analyses prove that the surfaces of the blocks had absorbed from the air and water at least 0.03, and sometimes as high as 0.14 of carbonic acid, the centre of the blocks absorbing only from 0.01 to 0.05. As the blocks were all in a state of perfect preservation, the minimum of surface absorption 0.03 was sufficient to preserve the interior; this gives 0.02 as the average minimum absorption requisite for preservation. The total quantity of lime being 0.35, the absorption of carbonic acid necessary for protection would be 21 lbs. per cubic yard of beton, containing 296 lbs. of lime.

To solve the question, as to whether Teil hydraulic lime would be able to form in the Atlantic Ocean or the British Channel, its protecting crust of carbonate of lime, it is necessary to examine what has occurred in mortars, in localities where the carbonic acid is in small quantities ; at several points on the western coast of France, Bayonne, etc., on the ocean, the proportion of carbonic acid is even greater than in the Mediterranean. In the analysis of beton blocks of Portland cement immersed in the British Channel, Rivot found that they had absorbed 0.017 of carbonic acid to 0.23 of lime. In a cubic yard of beton were 556 lbs. of cement, containing 494 lbs. of lime, which absorbed 37 lbs. of carbonic acid. Supposing this figure to be reduced one-half, to account for the lesser interior absorption, a minimum of 18½ lbs. is obtained, which is nearly the amount of carbonic acid found necessary for the protection of Teil lime in the Mediterranean. It is safe, then, to conclude that on the Atlantic coast of France, Teil lime will find sufficient carbonic acid for its protection, and it is presumable that the same will be the case on the Atlantic coast of the United States.

Plants and Shells.—The growth of marine plants, and the deposits of marine shells and incrustations on the surfaces of sea mortars and masonry, form the most efficacious protection that could be devised.

Storms and Currents.—Storms and sea currents disintegrate mortars by mechanical action ; as Teil lime has successfully resisted these causes of destruction in the Mediterranean, no special danger from their action need be feared in other localities.

Tides.—Tides are an advantage in the construction of marine works, and admit of part of the masonry being built dry at low tide ; this allows some time for mortars to set, and for their elements to complete all chemical reactions, which if they occurred after the setting would destroy the work. Slow-setting cements requiring from 8 to 18 hours to set are usually preferred in marine structures, but they are subject to the same inconvenience as Teil lime, in being covered by the tide before the setting is completed, unless special precautions be taken to protect the mortar or beton by a coating of quick-setting cement, or some other device. Teil hydraulic mortar sets strongly in 18 to 24 hours, and if it takes longer than some cements, its hardness once set rapidly equals theirs.

Teil hydraulic lime has been employed in the Mediterranean for all kinds of marine structures, in artificial blocks of beton dried during several months previous to immersion, and in beton immediately immersed in the sea for foundations. These betons have been equally durable, and there is no reason that it should be otherwise in tidal seas, where in any case precautions against washing away by the ebb and flood have to be provided, and where the temporary retreat of the sea renders the work of construction easier. The action of tidal currents on mortars is not different from that of river currents, in which Teil lime is daily employed in submarine works.

Economy of Teil Lime compared with Cements.—There remains the question of economy to be considered with regard to the use of Teil hydraulic lime instead of cements, such as Portland and others.

The claim for economy is based with justice upon two points: the comparative weights of Teil lime and cements, which are respectively about 1,200 pounds and 2,100 pounds per cubic yard, and the greater richness in silicate of lime, of Teil lime over an equal weight of cement.

For good sea mortars two conditions require to be fulfilled: *first*, each grain of sand should be coated with lime, and the voids filled; *second*, the proportion of silicate of lime, the most desirable element in hydraulic mortars, should not fall below a minimum quantity.

Chatoney and Rivot, in their examination of betons which had best resisted the action of the sea at Marseilles, found that 25 per cent. of the volume of the mortar was hydrosilicate of lime. This quantity, however, is not obligatory, as the hydraulic mortar used at Marseilles, in building the Napoleon Port, was 598 lbs. of Teil lime per cubic yard of sand, which corresponds to a proportion of 22 per cent. in volume of hydrosilicate of lime, and has given excellent results.

In hydraulic mortars, made either with Teil lime or Portland cement, the volume of lime or cement required to coat the grains of sand and fill the voids is equal in both cases. Owing to the greater density of Portland cement the weight required of the latter for the above volume will be greater, and per cubic yard of mortar will be about:

1,068 lbs. Portland cement (White Bros.)
1,070 " Boulogne Portland (Demarle.)
1011 " London Portland cement.

Whereas the same volume of Teil lime weighs 590 to 600 lbs. and works well in practice. If equal weights are employed instead of equal volumes, then the Portland cement will be only about one-half of what is required to fill the voids of the mortar.

With regard to the comparative richness in hydrosilicate of lime, of Teil lime and Portland cement mortars, by applying to the analyses of the latter the formulas of Chatoney and Rivot for hydration of silicates and aluminates of lime, and supposing the reactions completed, the following composition is obtained:

	English Portland.		Boulogne Portland.
Silicate of lime	60.3	....	58.5
Aluminate of lime........................	23.9	....	36.5
Free lime............................	14.9	....	4.3

Teil lime according to the same authorities contains on an average 66 per cent. of silicate of lime and 25 per cent. of free lime. This richness in silicate of lime gives Teil lime an advantage in any mortar for which a definite volume of lime or cement is required, and at an equal price per pound the economy of using the lesser weight per cubic yard of sand is clear.

If the quantity of silicate of lime is required to be equal in mortars made either with Teil lime or Portland cement, the weight of Teil lime will be considerably less than that of cement. Theory requires 598 lbs. of Teil lime to fill completely the voids of a cubic yard of sand; this weight contains 395 lbs. of silicate of lime. The weight required of Boulogne Portland cement, one of the best of slow-setting cements, to furnish an equal weight of silicate of lime is 674 lbs., which represents a volume of cement only $\frac{2}{3}$ of that required by theory for filling the voids of a cubic yard of sand.

These considerations show clearly that to make the employment of Teil lime and Portland cement equally economical, the latter must be lower in price than the former, or else the weight of Portland cement per cubic yard of mortar must be considerably diminished below that which would best fulfil the requisite conditions for good mortars.

The following comparative proportions are frequently employed of Teil lime and Portland cement for hydraulic mortars and betons.

Portland Cement.	Mortar:	cement ....840 lbs.	
		sand............$\frac{9}{10}$	cubic yards.
	Beton:	broken stone 1	"
		mortar ....$\frac{1}{2}$	"
Teil Hydraulic Lime. (Marseilles.)	Mortar:	lime............590 lbs.	
		sand ....$\frac{9}{10}$	cubic yards.
	Beton:	broken stone..0.93	"
		mortar.........0.58	"

The economy in the usual proportion of Teil lime instead of Portland cement is 250 lbs. per cubic yard of mortar, and admitting the same proportions of one of mortar to two of broken stone (which are often employed) for beton, the economy is 125 lbs. per cubic yard of beton. The saving may thus amount to 30 or 40 per cent.

Use of Teil Lime in Seaports, &c.—Teil hydraulic lime is now used in a large number of seaports. At the Universal Exhibition of 1867 specimens of Teil hydraulic mortars and betons in excellent preservation were exhibited from 22 seaports.

The chief ports where it is employed are: Marseilles (where in marine structures costing upwards of 50,000,000 francs Teil lime has been exclusively used), Toulon, Cette, Bordeaux, St. Malo, Cherbourg, Barcelona, Corsica, Algiers, Bona, Oran, Tunis, Genoa, La Spezzia, Trieste, Constantinople, Odessa, Suez and Port Said (120,000 tons of Teil lime), Alexandria Harbor Works (175,000 tons). It is also exported to La Plata, Rio Janeiro, Saigon, &c.

The following details respecting works in various ports, built of Teil lime, will be of interest.

Marseilles.—Teil hydraulic lime has been almost exclusively used at Marseilles during the last thirty-four years, by M. Pascal, the Chief Engineer, in the construction of the basins of La Joliette, Frioul, Napoleon, and the basins of the Marseilles docks and warehouses. It was employed as concrete for foundations and for artificial blocks for the protection of the seaward slopes of the breakwaters. The beton blocks were made in moulds and allowed to harden by exposure to the air for three months previous to immersion. The volume of each block was 353 cubic feet, with a weight of about 22 tons. The dimensions were $11' \times 5' \times 6\frac{1}{2}'$, and two grooves for suspension chains ran across the bottom. The composition of the mortar for concrete blocks was:

Teil lime in powder	3 parts in volume.
Sand	5 " "

The concrete was made of one volume of mortar mixed with two volumes of broken stone.

In concrete for immediate immersion, two volumes of mortar to three of broken stone were used.

M. Pascal considered that good hydraulic lime, for sea-mortars and concretes, was preferable to any mixture of lime and pozzuolana (sometimes added to hasten the setting), of lime and cements, or of natural and artificial cements.

For good work, sufficient time should be allowed for blocks to harden before immersion, and obtain their protecting crust of carbonate of lime.

The system of building quay walls at Marseilles, with blocks of

Teil concrete, was very successful. A bed of broken stone or gravel was formed on which four courses of artificial blocks were placed, their greatest length inwards forming the thickness of the wall (11 feet); the top course was 8 inches above the level of low tide. Divers were required to place the blocks which broke joints as in ordinary masonry. To guard against future settling when the masonry wall would be built on the blocks, the latter were temporarily loaded with two courses of similar blocks, which were removed when the settling was completed to the level of low tide. The blocks were of the volume, weight and composition previously mentioned. (Plate I.)

The construction of concrete blocks for the quay walls and breakwaters of Marseilles, required the establishment of large yards, covering 375 acres for machinery, workshops, tracks, supplies, and space for one thousand blocks in every stage of completion. The yard turned out monthly 300 to 375 blocks.

Toulon.—Teil hydraulic lime was employed in the works of the Port of Toulon; notably for 200,000 cubic yards of beton used in the construction of the three large graving docks of Castigneau. M. Noel and M. Raoul, Chief Engineers, state that Teil lime has perfectly resisted the action of the sea at Toulon, and also at Port Vendres, where large blocks for the jetty were made of limestone masonry cemented with Teil hydraulic lime mortar.

Algiers.—Since 1852 Teil lime is used in this port mixed with sea sand, for concrete immersed green, and for artificial blocks, which are allowed to harden in air from 2½ to 5 months according to the season. Teil concrete has shown great strength and resists the action of the sea at Algiers and other points along the coast. (See Appendix.)

Port Said.—The successful creation by M. de Lessèps of the artificial harbor of Port Said at the entrance of the Suez Canal, enclosing 90 acres of sea room, and with the basins 130 acres, is due in a great measure to the use of Teil lime, which allowed the project to be carried out without an expenditure which would have curtailed its dimensions, and endangered its success.

The two jetties, starting from points on the shore 1,530 yards apart, run out to sea, and approach each other within four hundred and forty yards. The length of the Western jetty, built first, as a protection from the prevailing winds, is 3,390 yards, and that of the Eastern jetty is 1,968 yards. The jetties are about 28 yards wide at the base and 6 at the summit, with a height of 10 yards at their seaward extremity. The summit of the jetties rises 6½ feet above the mean level of the Mediterranean Sea, and their slopes are at 45°.

In their construction, about 120,000 tons of Teil hydraulic lime were employed, chiefly in the fabrication of 25,000 artificial blocks of the same dimensions as those used at Marseilles. The volume of each block was 353 cubic feet, and the weight about 25 tons. The blocks were composed of:

Teil hydraulic lime in powder, 548 pounds.

Sand of the desert (almost impalpable), 1 cubic yard.

The mortar was mixed with sea-water, and poured into moulds, and after 2 to 3 months hardening in the air, the blocks were ready for immersion.

The above proportions correspond to 1 volume of lime to 2 of sand. The yard of fabrication contained from 2,000 to 3,000 blocks in various stages of preparation, and turned out 900 blocks monthly, 30 daily for immersion, by tipping into the sea from barges. The contractors were Messrs. Dussaud Bros., celebrated for their important marine constructions at Algiers, Marseilles, Cherbourg. The contract price of the blocks was 42 francs per cubic metre or $6.40 per cubic yard. The cost of each block in its final position was 1,000 francs, or $15.30 per cubic yard. Teil hydraulic lime and desert sand were also used in similar proportions to those employed for the artificial blocks, in building the Lighthouse of Port Said. The latter is 180 feet high, constructed of a single mass of beton with no joints, and rests on a beton base of about 400 cubic yards. (See Frontispiece.)

Alexandria.—The Harbor Works of Alexandria, Egypt, are in course of construction, and use an immense quantity of Teil lime;

they consist of a breakwater about 1½ miles long and an inner jetty, and quays; over 15,000 acres will be enclosed.

The breakwater will rise 10 to 15 feet above the mean level of the sea, and will be built on the Port Said plan, with artificial blocks. About 15,000 of these are made, and it is estimated that 35,000 blocks in all will be required, besides large quantities of rubble stone. The quantity of Teil lime used in this vast undertaking will be about 175,000 tons.

The concrete blocks are each 353 cubic feet in volume (10′ × 6′ × 6′) and about 20 tons in weight. Each block contains 34 cwt. of Teil hydraulic lime in powder mixed with desert sand and broken limestone (291¼ lbs. lime per cubic yard of concrete).

The concrete is mixed by 10 H. P. machinery on the upper platform of a travelling crane, stationed over the empty mould, which is filled from above. After a few days the frame sides of the mould are removed, and the block is left to harden for 2½ months. Forty blocks are ready daily and loaded on lighters, towed out to sea, and tipped on the site of the breakwater.

The yard of fabrication constantly contains about 2,500 blocks in course of preparation, in five long rows, running over nearly 1¼ miles of ground. It is well supplied with travelling cranes, 50 miles of railroad track, turn-tables, 12 locomotives, several hundred trucks, 40 steam engines, 12 lighters, six steamers, and one large steam derrick, representing about £200,000 sterling of capital, in plant alone. Two thousand Arabs are employed.

This undertaking, which equals in greatness that of Plymouth or Portland, will probably be completed in one-fifth the time. ("The Engineer.")

The contractors are Messrs. Greenfield & Co. (in reality Messrs. Kennard, Elliot & Maclean), Mr. May, Chief Engineer, and Mr. Brown, Chief Assistant Engineer.

General Observations.—Teil hydraulic lime has been exposed to the action of the sea for a long period of years, in some localities, since 1832, and there has been ample time and opportunity for any defects it may have to declare themselves. Far from this, Teil lime has uniformly given good results, and Vicat, Chatoney, and Rivot, speak of it in terms of high appreciation; the records in their reports show conclusively its remarkable durability in marine structures, and the Teil mortars examined are referred to as being in a state of excellent preservation.

It is considered preferable to use Teil lime alone in mortars or concretes, instead of in mixtures with other limes or cements, natural or artificial; pozzuolana is generally subject to great alteration in sea-water, and should be avoided in any case.

In June, 1856, M. Pascal, Chief Engineer at Marseilles, in a diving-bell, visited with the greatest care the Teil mortars and artificial blocks of the Port, chiefly the oldest, which were at a depth of 43 feet, and immersed from 7 to 9 years previously. His testimony is interesting; he says:

"The exterior blocks, the only ones I could see, are covered with a luxuriant vegetation, and their edges are perfectly sharp. An opening which I had occasion to make in the jetty, allowed me to visit a submerged block which did not show the slightest trace of vegetation, owing to the complete absence of light, and which was very hard and perfectly intact; the age of this block might be seven years. I also visited the concrete immediately immersed after fabrication about 7 or 8 years ago; this concrete was equally intact, but instead of a growth of marine plants, a thick deposit of 'serpules anhélides' was found. The thickness of these deposits runs up to 13¾ inches. Everywhere intact betons."

The great extension in the use of Teil lime for marine structures is chiefly due to the favorable results obtained in the works at Marseilles.

CANALS, SEWERS, AQUEDUCTS.

Teil hydraulic lime is used in the construction of the Forez Canal, France, and has given excellent results. (See Appendix.) It is very suitable for all kinds of work which require to be water-tight.

BRIDGES, RAILROADS, TUNNELS.

Teil lime has been used in large quantities for railroad constructions in France, and the engineers of several important roads speak highly of its value, in the most difficult parts of the works under their direction. (See Appendix.)

In the construction of the celebrated Mont Cenis Tunnel, upwards of 5,000 tons of Teil hydraulic lime were employed with very satisfactory results. (See Appendix.) It has been used in the construction of bridges, for the masonry of piers. At Constantine, in Algeria, the remarkable bridge of El-Kantara, with a span of 188¼ feet, has been built across a chasm 394 feet deep. The piers were built of limestone, cemented with Teil hydraulic lime; in the trial loading of the bridge, they were subjected during forty-eight hours, without showing any sign of weakness, to a crushing weight of 260 lbs. per square inch. During the construction of the piers, the temperature of the air was frequently 112° to 134° F. This heat would have destroyed by crumbling, many limes, but Teil mortar hardened rapidly under it and attained great strength.

WAREHOUSES, BUILDINGS, FOUNDATIONS, CELLARS.

Teil hydraulic mortar makes very good work in masonry for warehouses, buildings, etc., which, from their position, are subjected to more or less humidity. It makes an excellent coating instead of cement for masonry, and is particularly adapted to foundation work, cellars, cesspools, etc. Cornices of buildings are made of Teil lime.

ARTIFICIAL STONES.

In many localities artificial stones of various kinds are destined to a large consumption, from their cheapness as compared with stone brought from a distance, or ornamental cut stone for architectural purposes.

Beton Coignet, an artificial sandstone of great strength, is successfully used in all kinds of construction, from the carved work of a church window, to the foundations of a steam engine, a sewer, or an aqueduct. Teil lime has been employed in the fabrication of Beton Coignet, and experiments were made by M. Michelot, Engineer-in-Chief of the Ponts et Chaussées upon samples of the following composition:

Mixed sand....................................	4 to 5	volumes.
Teil or other hydraulic lime	1	"
Portland cement..............................	¼ to ¾	"

The results were a tensile strength of 288 to 426 lbs. per square inch, and a crushing weight of 2,634 to 7,495 lbs. per square inch.

Paris contains upwards of 31 miles of sewers of various sizes made of Beton Coignet, and there can be no doubt that with Teil lime, this excellent material for sewers can be made at a saving of at least 20 per cent. on common masonry. The Fontainebleau section of the Vanne Aqueduct, constructed to furnish Paris with water, is 37 miles long, made of fine sand, hydraulic lime, and a small proportion of cement, and is an instance of what can be built with this beton, when good ingredients are used.

In the manufacture of other artificial stones such as the *Frear Stone* (shellac, hydraulic cement and sand), or the *American Building Block Co.'s Stone* (unslaked lime mixed with moist sand), it may be found advantageous to mix a proportion of Teil hydraulic lime with the other ingredients. Whenever the quality of the stone depends on the use of a strong hydraulic lime or cement, Teil lime will give good results.

BRICKS AND SLABS FOR FLOORS, PARTITION WALLS, ETC.

Bricks and slabs made of pulverized blast furnace slags, mixed with a small proportion of Teil hydraulic lime, make a very light and strong material, which does not conduct sound, and will stand a heat of 1,000° C. without melting. This material, pressed into various shapes, is suitable for deafening floors, and for partition walls, fire-proof buildings, etc. It is best to use slags containing as little sulphur as possible, as sulphate of lime is injurious to the mixture, and cracks and fissures it.

CONCLUSION.

The preceding remarks on the applications of Teil hydraulic lime show to what extent it is already used in the various departments of engineering and construction. It fills the want which is felt in many localities for a good hydraulic material, and the experience already obtained of its durability is the best guarantee for the future.

In the Appendix will be found a brief account of the method and cost of fabrication of the artificial blocks of Teil concrete employed at Marseilles, and a number of certificates from engineers who have used Teil hydraulic lime in their works..

APPENDIX.

FABRICATION OF ARTIFICIAL BLOCKS OF TEIL BETON AT MARSEILLES.

General Description of the Yard of Fabrication.—The plant consisted of a steam engine of 15-horse power, which set in motion:

1. The wheels of three mortar mills.
2. A balance beam for elevating the ingredients to the floor of the mills.
3. The mixing cylinders for beton.
4. An hydraulic wheel for raising water from a well to wash the pebbles previous to use.

The floors of the mortar mills and mixing cylinders for beton were raised above the level of the yard. The materials, loaded into cars at the heaps, were run by a rail track A (Plate II.), upon a platform B, under the balance beam, which lifted them to the floor above, where by another rail track, running parallel to the mortar mills, the cars reached the latter, and the sand and lime were emptied into them.

The water for mixing mortar was contained in large tubs, fixed to the floor, and supplied by pipes connecting with the city mains.

The mortar, having been mixed, was expelled from the mills through an aperture in the bottom of the trough, kept closed by a valve during the mixing, and fell into a special car, placed beneath the mill under the centre of the valve.

The car by the turn-table, C, and the lower rail track, D, was run upon the platform of the balance beam, and lifted to the floor of the mills, where the rail track, E, directed it to the small shutes, under which were stationed the mixing cylinders for beton, with their covers open. The car was tipped, and its contents directed into the mixing cylinder by the shute.

The elevation of the mortar cars was followed by that of the pebble cars, arriving on the platform of the walking beam by the track D from the water wheel. The pebbles were emptied in the same way as the mortar, into the beton cylinders, which then contained the necessary ingredients for a mixing of beton.

The empty sand and lime cars were lowered to the yard on the platform of the steam balance beam, and, to avoid crowding, the empty mortar and pebble cars were lowered by a balance beam worked by a windlass, and situated at the opposite end of the floor.

The ingredients in the mixing cylinders were intermixed by the rotary motion communicated to each cylinder by a belt from a line of shafting.

When the mixing was completed the beton cylinder on its travelling frame was run by a short cross track upon a truck, which carried it by a lower rail track to the head of the line of blocks in fabrication. This line was formed by successive box moulds, upon the top of which was established a movable rail track. This track was continued onwards as the line of blocks progressed. The beton cylinder was run on the movable track over the mould to be filled, emptied of its contents, and run back to the mixing platform by the way it came. The size of the finished block was 3.40 metres long by 2.00 metres wide, and 1.50 metres high.

The beton having attained a sufficient degree of hardness, the blocks were fit for immersion. Longitudinal ties with rails were laid on the ground on each side of the line of blocks to be lifted; on this temporary track a travelling crane approached, lifted the block, and transported it to a truck running on a cross rail track F leading to the shipping wharf. A derrick lifted the block and deposited it on the deck of a lighter, which transferred it to the point of use. Some details of the methods of fabrication of the beton and handling will be useful.

Fabrication of the Mortar. Proportions.—The mortar was composed of 3 parts of screened lime in powder to 5 parts of sand, uncompacted, and corresponding in weight to 632 lbs. of lime per cubic yard of sand, which formed one mixing of mortar (300 kilog. lime to 0.80 cubic metre of sand; proportions used in the construction of La Joliette and Le Frioul ports).

Various sands were employed; pure sea-sand, pudding-stone sand, and quarry sand. The two latter qualities contained, as shown by washing, from 12 to 18 per cent. of foreign matter such as earths and clays.

In these conditions the quantity of water required for mixing the lime into paste varied with the quality of the sand; with sea-sand about 6 U. S. gallons of water per 100 lbs. of lime were used, and with earthy or clayey sand 9 to 9½ gallons were required.

The above proportions of mortar after mixing gave an increase in volume of:

5 per cent. for mortar made with sea-sand.
7 " " " pudding-stone sand.
6 " " " ravine or quarry sand.

The sand was measured in *iron cars* of the exact volume (0.80 cubic metre) required for one mixing of mortar. (Plate V.) The lime was in sacks sealed with lead, and of an average weight of 50 kilog. or 110¼ lbs., and the necessary quantity of lime was obtained by taking a certain number of sacks without further weighing. The water was measured in buckets of known capacity.

On the ground floor of the mortar mill building were the rail-tracks and turn-tables for the handling of the cars, the steam engine, and the lines of shafting for setting in motion the mortar mills, the hydraulic wheel for washing the pebbles, and the beton cylinders. On the upper floor, which consisted of a platform raised 10½ feet above the ground and supported by timber posts, were established three mortar mills.

Each *mortar mill* (Plates III., IV.) consisted of a circular cast-iron trough of trapezoidal section in which revolved three wheels and a scraper, fastened to the ends of four axles at right angles to each other, and dividing the surface of the trough into quarters.

The wheels were placed at unequal distances from the centre of the mill, and in such a manner that the sum of their several widths of tire was equal to the width of the bottom of the trough; thus a wheel ran always tangent to each side of the trough, whilst the third wheel ran on the middle of the bottom.

The scraper was formed of three curved wings reaching to the bottom of the trough, and fixed above to a cross-bar of iron at the extremity of the fourth axle.

From a ring fastened above the iron bar, the hook of a sheet-iron scraper was suspended, at the end of each mixing, for cleaning the trough. The section of the sheet-iron scraper was equal to that of the trough, and by means of a handle a downward pressure was exerted on the scraper, to drive it into the mortar, and to force the latter over the opening of a trap-door in the bottom of the trough, kept closed during the mixing, and through which the mortar was expelled into a car below.

The rotary motion of the mortar mills was obtained by bevelled gearing on the horizontal main shaft driven by the steam engine, and on the vertical shafts, running through the centres of the mills, to which were fastened the axles of the wheels and scraper.

Each mill produced in one mixing 0.84 cubic metre (1.10 cubic yard) of mortar, and the time required was from 15 to 20 minutes. The three mills produced 17 cubic yards of mortar per hour. In the fabrication of the mortar, the lime was first emptied into the trough of the mill and equally spread out; sufficient water was added to form a soft paste, and the sand was then thrown in and the whole mixed. Fifty-nine gallons of water were generally used for one mixing.

The *iron cars* which received the mortar (Plate VII.) were subdivided into three equal compartments, each 0.28 cubic metre in volume (9.89 cubic feet), so that each car contained a full mixing of mortar, inclusive of the increase in volume of the latter.

Fabrication of the Beton and Blocks. Proportions.—The beton was composed of five volumes of broken stone and three volumes of mortar.

To obtain these proportions, the volume of a stone car was made 0.465 cubic metre (16.42 cubic feet), and its contents, when mixed with one of the compartments of a mortar car, 0.28 cubic metre, corresponded to 0.50 cubic metre of beton (17.66 cubic feet). The mixing of the broken stone and mortar was accomplished in six horizontal sheet-iron *cylinders* (Plate VIII.) rotating on their axes, and placed on four-wheeled trucks or travelling frames, for transportation on the rail tracks. The cylinders were placed on a floor beneath that of the mortar mills, at a height sufficient to allow of the ingredients for concrete being run into them by shutes or inclined planes from the upper floor. On the platform were six rail tracks, which ran across it.

The mortar car, from under the mortar mill, after being directed by the turn-table and the lower rail track to the elevator, was lifted to the upper floor, and run upon a track which was laid adjoining the shutes, ten in number, leading to the beton cylinders. The mortar car was stopped in front of the first shute, into which the contents of one of the compartments were emptied, and thus directed into a beton cylinder below; the contents of each of the other two compartments were emptied in the same way into the next two shutes leading to beton cylinders.

The elevation of a mortar car was followed by that of three cars filled with washed pebbles, which were in succession emptied into the beton cylinders which had received the mortar.

A second mortar car, followed by three cars of broken stone, were then lifted, and emptied in the same way; the filling of the six cylinders in use for mixing beton was thus completed.

After each filling, the empty cars were lowered to the yard and re urned for a fresh supply of mortar, pebbles, and broken stone.

The pebble cars, when filled, were placed under the water spout connected with the water wheel, and the pebbles thoroughly washed.

The *cars* used in the transportation of these materials (Plate VI.), consisted of a box carried by a four-wheeled truck. The box was kept in equilibrium on a longitudinal axis, by means of a cross rod attached by rings to the bottom of the box. The rod ended in a hook at the front of the car, and kept closed one of the sides of the box; this side acted as a movable door hinged on its upper rim. At the back of the car the rod, was ended by a hook catching on a peg fixed to the truck. By a sudden movement given to the rod, the equilibrium of the car was destroyed, the side door opened, and the contents emptied.

The mixing machines having been filled, a rotary motion was communicated to each cylinder by a belt passing around a small pulley on the axis of the cylinder, and a second pulley on an intermediate line of shafting which ran the whole length of the platform, and was driven by a cogged connection with the main shaft of the mortar mills. To put the mixing in operation, the beton cylinders were backed from the shutes sufficiently to tighten the belts on the pulleys, and then kept in position by blocking the wheels of the frames or trucks.

The volume of a mixing of beton, as previously settled, was to be 0.50 cubic metre (17.66 cub. ft.), and mixing cylinders of 0.75 cubic metre (26.49 cub. ft.) capacity were considered at first to be large enough; but it was found necessary to increase the volume of the mixing cylinders to 1.00 cubic metre (35.32 cub. ft.), in order to obtain sufficient room for the ingredients to intermix, by detaching themselves from the sides of the cylinder. The interior space of the cylinder was, moreover, divided by 12 radial arms riveted to the shaft and sides, for the purpose of more completely dividing and mixing the ingredients. (Plate VIII.) Twenty revolutions of the cylinders, at a moderate speed, were sufficient to effect a proper mixing of beton. The speed should be moderate, otherwise the ingredients, by virtue of the centrifugal force, would adhere to the sides of the cylinder without intermixing.

To regulate this part of the fabrication, which would be impossible if the number of revolutions had to be counted by the eye, a mechanical counter was provided. It consisted of a sheet-iron disc attached to the fixed frame of the mixing machine, and capable of revolving around a ring screw on its axis. The circumference of the disc was divided into 20 parts by triangular notches, thus forming an equal number of teeth less one which was replaced by a notch. An index fixed to the beton cylinder, at each revolution of the latter, pressed on one of the teeth, and advanced the disc one turn; after 20 revolutions, if the disc was properly placed at the start, the index turned free in the notch replacing the tooth which had been suppressed ; this indicated that the required number of turns had been accomplished. The blocking wedges were withdrawn from the wheels, the belt was loosened, and the beton cylinder ceased revolving. A mixing of beton lasted 5 minutes.

The travelling frame carrying the cylinder was run on to rails placed upon the platform of a truck, which transported it by a rail track to the head of the line of blocks in fabrication. The rails on the platform of the truck were on the same level as the rails on the floor of the mixing cylinders, and as the rails of the movable rail track set upon the blocks.

The frame carrying the beton cylinder was run upon the movable track, until it was stopped over the box mould which was to be filled. The cover of the beton cylinder was then opened, the latter turned half round on its axis, and the beton emptied into the mould below. The cylinder was then righted, and with open cover returned to the floor for another mixing.

The beton emptied into the mould was sufficient to cover the surface to a depth of 5½ inches. This layer was equalized and firmly packed by three workmen provided with shovels, and rammers of 31 lbs. weight.

As each beton cylinder contained ½ cubic metre of beton, it required 21 loads to fill a mould, taking into account the settling and compacting of the beton, which was 5 per cent. The fabrication of a block generally occupied an hour.

The pannels of the box-moulds rested on close-jointed wooden flooring which formed the bottom of the moulds. Across the bottom, and at about 0.50 metre from the ends, small hollow boxes of slats were placed, to form grooves in the block for the suspension chains used in handling. The lower grooves were continued vertically up the sides of the blocks. These side grooves were obtained by timbers of trapezoidal section, slightly fastened to the pannels of the moulds, and separated from the beton when the moulds were taken apart.

In the fabrication of the blocks, no voids were allowed in the interior, and the surfaces were required to be perfectly smooth, and to present the appearance of a coat of mortar.

The first of these conditions was fulfilled by ramming. The second was obtained by throwing the beton violently against the interior sides of the pannels ; the mortar alone adhered to the latter, the pebbles, etc., being thrown back. The surfaces of the finished block presented no sign of broken stone or pebbles. The upper surface of the block was smoothed with the shovel when the mould was completely filled.

In consequence of the ramming and of the weight of the beton before the setting took place, it sometimes happened that the pannels of the moulds were forced out of shape, and the blocks also. These deformations arose from the swelling of the vertical pannels, and the swelling prevented subsequently the blocks from being placed close together in building the courses of quay walls. This disadvantage was partly obviated by tightening bolts applied to the top and bottom of the moulds, and by bracing the pannels from the outside, when a neighboring line of blocks allowed it to be done.

The object of the vertical grooves left in the blocks during their fabrication was, to permit the suspension chains to lodge in them ;

without this precaution, the thickness of the chains would, of necessity, have obliged the blocks to be left considerably apart in building them into the courses of a quay wall.

The moulds were taken to pieces three days after completion of the filling; at this age the beton had acquired sufficient consistency to hold together, and to bear the weight of the movable rail track set on top, and used for running the beton cylinders back and forth. The blocks thus exposed to the air, remained in the yard during the time required for their complete drying and hardening. The length of time required varied from 40 to 50 days, according to the season. Sometimes blocks have been lifted and transported to the point of use in 29 days after fabrication.

The putting together and taking apart of the box moulds was easily accomplished. The moulds consisted of two side and two end pannels, joined together simply by juxtaposition, and kept in place by iron bolts, on one end of which a screw thread was cut, and a nut with a handle used for tightening. The taking apart consisted in loosening the nuts, and removing the separate pannels.

Lifting, Loading, and Transportation of the Blocks.— The lines of blocks in the yard ran parallel to each other, and were separated by a clear space of about 2 feet. The thickness of the sides of the moulds rendered this space necessary in any case, and it was also required for the movable rail track used in the transportation of the blocks.

The lifting and transporting of the blocks was effected by a *steam travelling crane.* (Frontispiece.)

The crane consisted of a strong sheet iron frame, 19½ ft. long by 9 ft. 2 in. wide, with 4 cast-iron wheels. The frame was divided by a sheet-iron partition into two compartments, the rear one with sheet-iron sides was empty and received the block; the fore compartment was covered with a floor upon which rested the steam engine, boiler and machinery. The engine was of 8 horse-power, vertical, non-condensing, with 2 cylinders and a tubular boiler.

A system of gearing transmitted the power, either to a vertical shaft which, by a cog-wheel on one of the axles, worked the travelling crane backward and forward, or else to a horizontal shaft which communicated the motion to two vertical screws used in lifting the blocks.

The travelling crane with its frame was carried by a truck with rails fixed on its platform. The truck travelled back and forth on the rail track G. (Plate II.) and placed the crane at the head of the different lines of blocks. The rails on the platform of the truck were on a level with the rails of the movable track established on the ground on each side of the blocks for the use of the travelling crane. The movable track consisted of heavy longitudinal oak ties carrying the rails.

When a line of blocks was ready for immersion, the travelling crane left the truck, and, passing across the sunken track F on to the movable track, approached the first block. The suspension chains, previously passed around the block and lodged in the grooves of the latter, were fastened to the ends of two horizontal beams, fixed to the lower part of the vertical screws. The beams consisted of two plates of sheet iron, strengthened and connected by iron braces; at their extremities a hole was cut for the key which held the end of the chain, and the beams, like the arms of a pair of scales, worked on a pivot at the point of fastening to the vertical screws, in order to be more easily attached to the chains.

The chains being attached, the horizontal shaft, extending the whole length of the upper part of the frame of the crane, was set in motion; on this shaft were two sections of an endless screw, which engaged with two horizontal pinions bearing teeth on their outer circumference, and through the centres of which passed the upright ends of the hoisting screws. The pinions formed the nuts of the screws, and as the former were prevented from rising, the latter were forced to ascend, carrying the block up with them. The travelling crane then transported the block over the sunken track F, and deposited it upon a truck below. To free the block, which was still surrounded by the sides of the crane, the latter moved on to the travelling frame or truck, on the outer track G, drawing after it by a hook and chain, the two girders forming a bridge across the sunken track, and which would have interfered with the passage of the truck loaded with the block. When the latter had moved away, the bridge girders were replaced, and the travelling crane returned across them to obtain another block.

The block was transported along the lower rail track, under a scaffold or derrick established on the shore; on the upper girders of the derrick a travelling windlass lifted the block and deposited it on a lighter. The loaded truck with the block was either drawn by an endless chain from a stationary steam-engine beneath the derrick, or else by a small locomotive, and later by horses.

The lighters were towed to the point of use by a steamer. They were generally made of the hulks of old sailing vessels, of which the deck was lowered. Three blocks were loaded on each lighter.

Employment of Artificial Blocks.—The blocks were used in protecting the seaward slope of the jetties, and also in the construction of quay walls. (Plate I.)

Jetties.—In the revetment of the jetties the blocks were used below and above the level of the sea, and the operation of placing them was different in each case.

Blocks Used Beneath the Level of the Sea.—The lighters used in transporting blocks to be sunk in the sea were prepared as follows: On the deck was established an incline capable of receiving 3 blocks, and on the timbers forming the ways, strongly greased pine skids were placed; a horizontal iron rod lay on the deck along the foot of the skids, and was kept in place at each end by two rings, through which it passed. To the rod were fixed 6 iron arms, two by two, so that two arms were in front of each block on the ways. At each end of the iron rod was a handle in the same plane with the iron arms, with which the rod could be turned in the rings. Before loading the lighter the handles were lifted upright, and kept in that position by a catch attached to the deck; the iron arms also were then vertical.

The blocks were lowered upon the ways, and kept in position by the iron arms against which they rested. When the lighter had reached the point of immersion, the catch holding the handles was let go, and the iron arms, being no longer retained in position, were forced over on to the deck by the weight of the blocks, which then slid off the lighter into the sea.

Blocks used above the Level of the Sea.—The blocks were deposited on a lighter, the deck of which was level, and towed to the point of use, where a floating derrick or sheers on a barge awaited them. The summit of the sheers reached 5.00 metres (16½ ft.) beyond the bow of the barge. A windlass, with a 10-horse power engine, worked a heavy iron chain over a pulley at the end of the sheers. The chain ended in four smaller chains, capable of being fastened together two by two.

The sheers and lighter being in proximity, the chains were passed around in the grooves of a block, the windlass set in motion, and the blocks suspended in air. By hawsers from the jetty, the barge and sheers were hauled in front of the point to be covered, and the block was lowered upon the slope of the jetty. The main chain was slackened, the small chains unfastened from the block, and the operation completed.

The placing of a block by this method occupied about 20 minutes, and in calm weather up to 31 blocks could be placed in a day, and generally 25 blocks. High tide was preferred for immersion, as the chances of breakage of the blocks were diminished by the greater thickness of water they had to pass through.

Quay Walls.—The general foundation of the jetty, etc., consisted of a bank of broken stones of various sizes, à pierre perdue, rising from the bed of the sea, at a depth of 17 metres (56 ft.). On the interior slope of the jetty, the bank was carried up at 45° to within about 6 metres (19½ ft.) of the level of the sea. At this depth it formed a wide bench or set-back, upon which the quay wall, composed of four courses of beton blocks, each 1.50 metres (5 ft.) high, was built up to the level of the sea.

The surface of the bench was too irregular to serve as a bed for the blocks, and it was levelled by filling up the inequalities and spaces between the large stones, with small gravel and broken stones.

For this purpose, a raft of wood was anchored over the site of the quay. In the floor of the raft, a rectangular aperture was made, with its longest sides in the direction of the width of the set-back. On one of the longer sides a plank apron was erected, inclined towards the opening. On the opposite side was a vertical apron of boards.

A lighter loaded with small broken stones and gravel was moored to the raft, and the materials were emptied in small quantities upon the inclined apron, and through the opening in the floor of the raft, into the sea. A workman standing behind the vertical apron to protect himself from the splashing of the water, directed with a sounding lead the levelling of the bed of the quay. The rough bed was equalized over a width of 8 metres (26 ft.), corresponding to the length of a block 3.40 metres (11.16 ft.), with an additional width of 2.50 metres (8 ft.) in front. (Plate I.) The diving-bell was used for removing any pieces of rock, which from their large size interfered with the regularity of the bed.

These preparations being completed, the blocks were loaded on lighters, towed to the site, and suspended in air by the floating sheers, in the same way as when used for the seaward revetment. To lower the block to its bed, 6 metres below the surface of the water, and to align it in the quay wall, an iron frame was used, consisting of 3 sides, each 2.00 metres (6½ ft.) long, and equal to the width of the block.

At each angle of the iron frame sockets were placed, in which were clamped upright wooden posts 6 metres high. When the block was ready to be lowered the frame was placed upon it, the two uprights being in the same plane with that side of the block destined to form part of the face of the wall.

When the block was submerged and directed into its proper place by the frame and uprights, its position below was indicated by the visible portion of the latter above water; it was thus sufficient to place the uprights in the alignment of the proposed quay wall, to be certain that the blocks were also in it. When a block was placed the suspension chains were withdrawn, as well as the iron frame, which was kept in position only by its weight.

The placing of the first course of blocks was the most difficult to accomplish, on account of the occasional unevenness of the bottom, caused either by the action of the waves, or by imperfect levelling; divers were then employed to remove the obstacles.

The joints of the blocks of each course were laid as close as possible, and the joints of two successive courses were crossed at half the width of the block. To complete a course, blocks were cut to the required dimensions for filling the vacant space.

The wall of beton blocks was continued above water by masonry which formed the quay wall proper. To avoid the disruption of the latter by any settling of the blocks from the additional weight, they were previously loaded during several months with two courses of blocks. The settling produced by this weight was frequently very irregular, and the consequent inequalities in the surface of the upper course of blocks were carefully levelled with layers of cement concrete at the level of low tide, from which point the quay wall of masonry was built up. The bench of 2.50 metres in width, at the base of the wall of artificial blocks, was generally destroyed, in part by the united effects of the weight of the wall and the action of the waves; it was re-established with broken stones and rocks placed by the workmen in the diving-bells.

Personnel and Labor required.

1º. Fabrication.

Steam Engine.	Engineer and fireman.........	2	men.
Pebbles.	Loading cars..............................	12	"
	Washing..................................	7	"
Sand.	Loading cars..............................	6	"
	Conducting cars to elevator...........	2	"
	Unloading and heaping sand.........	3	"
Lime.	Loading cars and conducting to elevator..................	2	"
Floor of Mortar Mills.	Lifting cars...........	1	"
	Receiving lime and sand cars, and mill work.............................	6	"

Emptying mortar and pebble cars into beton cylinders.................. 5 men.

Lowering empty cars.................. 2 "

Floor of Beton Cylinders. Fabrication........ 2 "

Loaded and Empty Cars under Mortar Mill Floor.

Receiving mortar from mills.......... 2 "

Conducting mortar and pebble cars to elevator.............................. 5 "

Receiving empty cars lowered from mill floor.............................. 2 "

Transportation of Beton, Ramming, Moulds.

Transportation of beton................ 9 "

Ramming beton (3 men per mould) 9 "

Putting up and taking moulds apart. 8 "

(3 Beton Cylinders in Transportation. 3 Beton Blocks in Fabrication.)

2º. Lifting Blocks and Shipping.

Steam Crane. Engineer and fireman........... 2 "

Lifting and Shipping. Placing movable tracks, and service of blocks...10 "

Transporting blocks to shipping derrick (2 H. P. locomotive)........... 2 "

Lifting block at derrick, and loading on lighter.............................. 6 "

3º. Transportation to Point of Immersion.

Tow-boat. Officers and crew..................... 8 "

4º. Employment of Blocks under Water.

Number of lighters (1 loading, 1 transporting)......................... 2 lighters.

Labor in immersing...................... 8 men.

5º. Employment of Blocks for Crowning Jetties or Quay Wall Foundations.

Number of lighters for transporting 2 lighters.

Floating sheers......................... 1 sheers.

Labor on sheers......................... 7 men.
Crews of lighters, and labor in immersing................................ 6 "

Average Daily Production and Work.

Fabrication................................12 blocks.
Employment of blocks under water..20 "
Employment of blocks, crown of jetties..................................16 "
Employment of blocks, quay wall foundations..............................12 "

Description of a Smaller Yard of Fabrication.—The establishment of the plant described above entails a great expenditure, which can only be entered upon when a large quantity of beton is required. A smaller plant was established for the fabrication of 25,000 cubic metres (33,000 cubic yards) of beton to be immersed green for the graving docks of the port of Marseilles.

The plant consisted of a mortar mill for the fabrication of mortar, and a platform of planks on which the mixing of the mortar with the broken stones for beton was carried on. The wheels of the mortar mill were set in motion by a locomobile, which also worked a water-wheel for washing the pebbles.

The pebbles were deposited upon the platform in a long narrow heap of triangular section, and upon them was laid the proper quantity of mortar. The mixing was done by hand; three men with hoes on one side of the heap spread out the ingredients towards them on the board flooring, and were assisted by three men with shovels upon the opposite side. Two of the latter assisted in spreading out the mixture, whilst the third shovelled it over into a heap. The process of turning over was continued three times, and the beton was then sufficiently mixed. The beton in its passage across the platform, from its first to its third position, traversed during the mixing a distance of 6 metres, or about 6½ feet for each turning over.

The mortar on account of the peculiar character of the works in which it was to be used, was made with 400 kilog. of lime of Teil to 1.07 cubic metre of uncompacted sand (630 lbs. lime per cubic yard of sand). The beton consisted of three parts of pebbles to two parts of mortar.

The pebbles were transported to the platform in wheel-barrows, of which the volume was 2.37 cubic feet. The bottom of the barrows consisted of open work, to let the water run completely off, after washing the pebbles in the barrows.

The mortar was transported on barrows with a raised edge upon three sides, so as to give a volume of 1.59 cubic feet. The cubic contents of the pebble and mortar barrows were thus in the proportion of 3 to 2, and to avoid confusion, a barrow full of pebbles deposited on the mixing area was always followed by a barrow full of mortar, before the arrival of the next barrow of pebbles.

The beton made as above, was shovelled into sheet iron semi-cylindrical boxes for immersion. The boxes were placed on boats and transported to the point of use, where they were lifted by a crane set upon the caissons, and lowered into the water to form the hearting of the sea wall.

The daily fabrication was 60 cubic metres of beton.

The labor required for this production was:

	Steam Engine	1 man.
	Transportation of sand	4 men.
	do. of lime and work at mill	4 "
Pebbles.	Loading barrows and washing	10 "
	Returning barrows to platform	1 man.
	Loading mortar barrows, and emptying mortar on pebbles	8 men.
	Mixing beton (two gangs of men)	12 "
	Loading beton into boxes	5 "
	Transporting boxes by boat (3 boats and 3 boxes per boat)	9 "
Immersion.	Windlass	4 "
	Emptying boxes	2 "

Cost of Fabrication of Teil Beton Blocks.—In the important works of the construction of the Napoleon Basin and Jetty at Marseilles in 1857, of which M. Pascal was Chief Engineer, and MM. Dussaud Bros. Contractors, 10,000 artificial blocks of Teil beton were employed; the volume of each block was 10 cubic metres, 353 cubic feet.

The cost of fabrication, although lower than what it would be today, is interesting as giving the relative cost of the different items, and the proportions of beton.

Teil Beton for Artificial Blocks. (Marseilles.)

286½ lbs. of Teil lime at 28 fr. per ton	$0 73
Weighing, transporting and storage of lime	0 08
0.45 cubic yard of sand at 3.82 fr. per cub. yd.	0 35
1 cub. yd. of pebbles at 2.68 fr. per cub. yd.	0 53
Fabrication, inclusive of taking moulds apart, cost of moulds, &c., and groove boxes	0 46
Lifting, transporting, immersing, inclusive of cost of plant	0 46
General expenses $\frac{1}{20}$	0 09
Profit of contractor $\frac{1}{10}$	0 19
Cost* per cubic yard of artificial block in final position	$2 89

Teil Beton for immediate immersion. (Marseilles.)

337 lbs. of Teil lime at 30 fr. per ton	$0 92
0.54 cub. yd. of sand at 3.44 fr. per cub. yd.	0 37
0.90 cub. yd. of broken stone at 2.68 fr. per cub. yard	0 48
Fabrication and immersion	0 61
General expenses $\frac{1}{20}$	0 12
Profit of contractor $\frac{1}{10}$	0 25
Cost per cubic yard of beton immersed green	$2 75

Since the execution of these important works, the cost of Teil hydraulic lime has considerably increased, owing to its demand for works such as those of the Suez Canal, Alexandria Harbor, etc.

* All prices and costs given in gold.

In the construction of the Port Said Breakwaters, in 1865 to 1868, the cost of Teil beton per cubic yard of artificial block was $6.40 ; the cost of the block in final position was $15.30 per cubic yard.

The cost of fabrication by machinery of Teil beton for artificial blocks, at any point near New York, may be estimated as follows, adopting the proportions actually employed by French engineers of 590 lbs. Teil hydraulic lime per cubic yard of sand, producing 1.10 cubic yards of mortar, and one volume of Teil mortar to two volumes of broken stone. Teil hydraulic lime costs $21.75 per ton, delivered in dock, New York ; the cost of sand, broken stone, and labor is based upon the results obtained by General Gillmore in 1870 to 1871, in making concrete for the Staten Island Forts :

Teil Beton for Artificial Blocks. (*New York.*)

266 lbs. Teil lime, at $21.75 per ton of 2,240 lbs....	$2 58
1.45 cub. yds. of sand, at 36c. per cubic yard.......	0 16
0.50 cubic yard Teil mortar.	
1 " " of broken stones and pebbles. at $2.00 per cubic yard	2 00
Fabrication of beton (mixing, transporting to moulds, ramming), inclusive of taking moulds apart, cost of moulds, etc., and groove boxes......	1 60
Cost of Teil beton per cubic yard of block............	$6 34
Lifting, transporting, immersing, inclusive of cost of plant	2 00
General expenses $\frac{1}{20}$..	0 42
Profit of contractor..	0 88
Total cost per cubic yard of artificial block in final position..	$9 64

In betons made with Portland cement, it is a common practice to cheapen the product by employing equal volumes of cement and slaked ground non-hydraulic lime in powder, instead of cement alone.

With Portland cement alone, weighing 106 lbs. to the bushel, it is expensive to fulfil the conditions of a good mortar by filling the voids in the sand, and the use of the common lime is to remedy the lack of volume of the cement at the expense of homogeneity, and of a better resistance to the action of sea-water.

The opinion is gaining ground among many engineers, that it is preferable to employ a single lime or cement at a time in a mortar or beton instead of various mixtures, and that a good hydraulic lime used by itself is better than a mixture of a good cement and an ordinary lime, or of an ordinary lime and pozzuolana.

Teil lime weighing 56 lbs. to the bushel, gives not far from double the volume of the same weight of Portland cement. It is strongly hydraulic, very uniform in composition, and as its quality is invariable, Teil lime produces very homogeneous mortars and betons, which resist the action of sea-water.

For artificial blocks for marine structures, a beton of first rate quality can be made as above mentioned, for $6.34 per cubic yard of finished block. The same beton, in which the Teil lime, weighing 266 lbs., has been replaced by an equal volume of Portland cement, weighing 504 lbs. (at $20.60 per gross ton), would cost, the other items remaining the same, $8.39 per cubic yard of finished block, showing an increased cost of about 30 per cent.

If one-half of the volume of Portland cement is replaced by a common lime (252 lbs. of cement, at $20.60, and 178 lbs. of lime at $5 per gross ton), the other items remaining the same, the economy obtained by the use of Teil beton is about $0.14 per cubic yard, the prices of both betons being respectively $6.48 and $6.34 per cubic yard of block. In this case the chief advantage attending the use of Teil hydraulic lime, is that a more reliable and homogeneous beton is obtained, which can be depended upon to resist the action of the sea.

CERTIFICATES.

Port of Marseilles. (Mediterranean Sea.)

1. Teil lime, from the quarries of Messrs. L. and E. Pavin de Lafarge, has been employed for upwards of 16 years in the department of Bouches-du-Rhone. It has been used almost exclusively in the construction of La Jolliette and of the Frioul, notably in the fabrication of artificial blocks for the exterior slope of the jetties where they would receive the shock of the waves, and in the masses of concrete for the foundations of quay walls. The concrete in the artificial blocks was immersed after a preliminary drying in air for several months; the masses of concrete for foundations were immersed green.

All the works made with this lime have resisted perfectly the chemical action of salt water, and the shock of the waves. Of the great number of mortars made of various hydraulic limes on which we have experimented to determine the tensile strength, those made of Teil lime occupy the first place. Teil mortars have been used both in fresh and salt water, in masonry and as a coating. In these uses we have also found them far superior to other hydraulic mortars.

The Engineer-in-Ordinary,
(Signed) Pascal.

Marseilles, 17*th Feb.*, 1855.

2. To-day, on the termination of the works of the Napoleon Basin and of those of the Marseilles Docks and Warehouses Basins, exclusively constructed with the hydraulic limes of Teil (Ardèche) derived chiefly from the quarrries of MM. Pavin de Lafarge, we can testify to the superiority of these limes.

The Engineer-in Chief,
(Signed) Pascal.

Marseilles, 13 *Feb.*, 1867.

3. The undersigned, Engineer-in-Chief of Bridges and Highways, charged with the direction of the works of the Port of Marseilles, certifies that since 1840 the hydraulic limes of Teil have been exclusively employed in these works, of which the value is about fifty millions, and that they have given the best results.

It was on account of these ascertained facts that in nearly all the great works of the Mediterranean Ports recourse was had to these limes.

We would mention Algiers, Port Said on the Suez Canal, and the Port of Trieste.

(Signed) PASCAL.

MARSEILLES, 25*th Nov.*, 1872.

4. I, the undersigned, Engineer in Ordinary of Bridges and Highways, in charge of the Works of the Second Maritime Division of the Bouches-du-Rhone, certify that the firm of Mathieu Couturier (now Soullier & Brunot), lessee of the Hydraulic Lime Quarry of "Detroit," situated in the Commune of Teil (Ardèche) and belonging to that Commune, has been allowed since the year 1858, simultaneously with MM. Pavin de Lafarge, to furnish the Teil hydraulic limes required for the Maritime Works of the Bouches du Rhone and that it has since that date received the adjudication of seven contracts for the Second Division as follows :

Dec. 22, 1859.	Construction of Draw-Bridge at Martigues	1,400	Tons.
Sep. 29, 1864.	Construction Graving Docks, Port of Marseilles	6,500	"
Aug. 14, 1866.	Completion of Sewers of Plombieres and Aygalades, Pt. of Marseilles	180	"
Oct. 24, 1868.	Construction Graving Docks, Port of Marseilles	2,200	"
Jan. 18, 1869.	Construction Graving Docks, Port of Marseilles	882½	"
Aug. 9, 1870.	Construction Graving Docks, Port of Marseilles	1,550	"
Aug 9, 1870.	Construction Second Draw Bridge on the Joliette Traverse	200	"
		12,912½	Tons.

I certify, moreover, that the firm Mathieu Couturier always fulfilled to the satisfaction of the Administration the obligations incurred by its contracts.

(Signed) DENANIEL.

MARSEILLES, *July* 23, 1872.

Countersigned by the Chief Engineer of the Maritime Works,

(Signed) PASCAL.

MARSEILLES, *July* 27*th*, 1872.

5. I, the undersigned, Ingénieur Ordinaire des Ponts et Chaussées, in charge of the Works of the First Maritime Division of the Bouches-du-Rhone, certify that the Association formerly known under the firm name of Couturier, Soullier & Co., and at present as Soullier & Brunot, which Association is lessee of the Hydraulic Lime Quarry of "Detroit," situated on the Commune of Teil (Ardèche), and belonging to that Commune (the said Association being represented successively before the Administration by M. Couturier and M. Soullier), has been allowed since the year 1858, simultaneously with Messrs. Pavin de Lafarge, to furnish the Teil Hydraulic Limes required for the Maritime Works of the Bouches-du-Rhone, and that the said Association has, since the said date, furnished a series of the said limes, destined for the works of the above-named First Division, of which the dates, objects, and quantities are enumerated as follows:

Adjudication, 15th July, 1858. Completion of the Belt Sewer of the Port of Marseilles.................................. 1200 Tons.

Adjudication, 13th Sept., 1859. Improvement of the Quays of the Joliette Basin, Marseilles............. 350 "

Adjudication, 9th July, 1861. Construction of the Quay Walls, Napoleon Basin, Marseilles.......... 2450 "

Adjudication, 17th June, 1862. Fabrication of Artificial Blocks. Completion of Napoleon Basin Jetty.. 4500 "

Adjudication, 12th May, 1864. Fabrication of Artificial Blocks for Jetties of Imperial Basin.......... 9700 "

From 1868 to 1871 various works at Port Ciotat (re-charging the seaward slope of the prolongation of the New Mole with artificial blocks. Underpinning repairs of quay wall of Old Mole, and of quay wall of the prolongation of New Mole. Reconstruction of part of quay wall of Old Mole; construction of a shelter for fishing boats in the Meadow Cove)..	210 Tons.
Adjudication of October 25, 1871 (approved by Ministerial decision the following 27th December), re-charging the seaward slope of the prolongation of the New Mole with artificial blocks..............	175 "
	18,585 Tons.

I certify, moreover, that MM. Couturier & Soullier have always fulfilled, to the satisfaction of the Administration, the obligations they had incurred towards it by undertaking to supply the above materials.

(Signed) ANDRÉ.

MARSEILLES, 24 *July*, 1872.

Countersigned by the Chief Engineer of the Maritime Works,

(Signed) PASCAL.

MARSEILLES, *July*, 1872.

Port Said. Suez Canal.

COMPAGNIE UNIVERSELLE
du
CANAL MARITIME DE SUEZ.

I, the undersigned, certify that the artificial blocks with which the great Jetties of Port Said were constructed, from 1865 to 1868, by MM. Dussaud Bros., Contractors, under the superintendence and inspection of the engineers of the Company, were made with the hydraulic lime of Teil of MM. L. & E. Pavin de Lafarge, and that with regard to quality, homogeneity, hardness, etc., etc., this lime has always given excellent results.

I certify, moreover, that during the three years of the construction of these works, the establishment of Lafarge fnrnished for them alone upwards of eighty thousand tons of lime.

For the President,

(Signed) Ch. A. De Lesseps.

Paris, 11th *January*, 1873.

Port of Toulon. (Mediterranean Sea.)

1. I certify that since more than 20 years that Teil hydraulic lime has been used in the works of the port of Tonlon, this lime has always given excellent results in sea-water as well as in fresh water or exposed to the air, and for coating masonry; that no alterations have ever been observed in the mortars made with this lime and used in sea-water; that in the works executed by the Navy at Port Vendres, blocks of masonry with Teil lime have been constructed, and that these blocks employed in the revetment of the mole have resisted perfectly both the shock of the waves and the chemical action of salt water.

The Engineer-in Chief of the Ponts et Chaussées, Director of the Hydraulic Works of the Navy,

(Signed) Noel.

Toulon, 10*th Feb.*, 1855.

2. The Engineer-in-Chief of the Ponts et Chaussées, Director of the Hydraulic Works of the Navy, certifies that, during the last 12 years, the hydraulic lime of Teil of MM. Pavin de Lafarge has been almost exclusively employed at the Port of Toulon for all marine structures, and particularly in the fabrication of 153,000 cubic metres of concrete for the three graving docks of Castigneau, and that it has always given good results and a notable economy over the use of pozzuolana.

The lime of Teil is also usually employed for the coating and the cornices of masonry, and behaves very well exposed to air. The result of a visit, which he has made recently, shows that the blocks of the Port Vendres Jetty, made of Teil mortar, have resisted the action of the sea perfectly, and that no perceptible alteration has been noticed in the works executed with Teil lime during the last 25 years at Toulon.

(Signed) RAOUL.

TOULON, 3*d Jan.*, 1867.

Port of Cette. (MEDITERRANEAN SEA.)

1. The undersigned, Engineer-in-Ordinary of the Ponts et Chaussées, certifies that the lime of Teil (Ardèche) is the only lime employed for the maritime works of the Port of Cette since 1852; the works constructed since that date show great hardness, and not the slightest trace of decomposition.

(Signed) SALVA.

CETTE, 12*th Jan.*, 1867.

2. The undersigned, Engineer of the Ponts et Chaussées, certifies that the lime of Teil derived from the establishment of MM. Couturier, Soullier & Co., has been employed in 1864 and 1865 for the fabrication of artificial blocks of beton, and for the submerged concrete of the foundations of the quays which were reconstructed in the Canal of Cette, and that it has given good results.

(Signed) SALVA.

CETTE, 6*th April*, 1867.

Port Vendres. (MEDITERRANEAN SEA.)

I, the undersigned, Alfred Pasqueau, Engineer of the Ponts et Chaussées, attached to the ordinary service of the Department of Pyrénées Orientales, and to the special service of the Port and Railroad of Port Vendres, certify that the artificial blocks of masonry made since 1844 with Teil-Lafarge hydraulic lime, for the construction and preservation of the mole of Port Vendres, are in a state of perfect preservation, and do not show any trace of disintegration. I certify, moreover, that the same lime has been almost exclusively employed in our service for the construction of masonry works of the Port Vendres Railroad, and of the Imperial Roads, and that it has always given excellent results, with regard to quickness in setting as well as to strength of the mortars made.

In belief of which I have written this certificate, to give value where it is due.

The Engineer in Ordinary,

(Signed) PASQUEAU.

PERPIGNAN, 10*th January*, 1867.

Port of Saint Malo. (BRITISH CHANNEL.)

The undersigned, Engineer-in-Chief, certifies that the mortars made of Teil lime and sea sand, used in the blocks of masonry, and immersed in the sea during 8 years at Saint Malo, are to-day very hard and in perfect preservation.

In belief of which this certificate has been delivered to M. de Lustrac.

The Engineer-in-Chief,

(Signed) BELLINGER.

SAINT MALO, 30*th August*, 1862.

Pointe-de-Grave. (BAY OF BISCAY, ATLANTIC OCEAN.)

The undersigned, Engineer in Ordinary, in charge of the defensive works of the Pointe-de-Grave, Department of the Girande, certifies as follows:

He had constructed during the month of March, 1860, five blocks, each 9 cubic metres in volume; three were made of ordinary masonry and two of beton, composed of three volumes of mortar to five of pebbles. The mortar used contained 4 kilogrammes of Teil lime furnished by M. Pavin de Lafarge, to 10 litres of sand.

These blocks were immersed on the Eastern slope of the Pointe-de-Grave jetty, at the end of the month of May, 1860; a scouring of the bed of the sea, which occurred on the 13th November, 1864, having caused them to disappear in the sea, where they were covered by other blocks, it is no longer possible to verify the state of preservation in which they are at present.

Previous to the 13th November, 1864, these five blocks, which had been on several occasions minutely examined, did not show any trace of decomposition.

In belief of which the undersigned delivers this certificate to M. Pavin de Lafarge, for him to use as he shall see fit.

(Signed) ROBAGLIA.

BORDEAUX, 22*d January*, 1867.

Port of Saint-Jean-de-Luz. (BAY OF BISCAY, ATLANTIC OCEAN.)

I, the undersigned, Engineer-in-Chief of the Ponts et Chaussées, in charge of the service of the maritime works of the Basses-Pyrénées and the Landes, certify that the mortar brick delivered to M. de Lustrac, agent of MM. Pavin de Lafarge, manufacturers of Teil lime, to be sent to the exhibition, was made on the 15th April, 1865, of a mixture of three parts in volume of sand to one part of Teil lime, derived from the establishment of MM. Pavin de Lafarge, and mixed with fresh water; that it was deposited on the 12th May, 1865, in the experimental bath of the Tour des Signaux, at the mouth of the Adour river, filled with sea-water renewed every eight days, and that it remained constantly immersed until this day.

I certify, moreover, that since 1865, Teil lime has been employed in the fabrication of small artificial blocks for the Sacoa breakwater, at the entrance of the bay of Saint-Jean-de-Luz, the actual state of which blocks cannot be ascertained, as they were used in the foundations and mixed with natural blocks and large artificial blocks of Portland cement mortar.

The Engineer-in-Chief of Maritime Works,

(Signed) DAGUENET.

BAYONNE, 2*d January*, 1867.

Port of Barcelona (MEDITERRANEAN SEA.)

1. D. José Rafo, Inspector generale de segunda clase del Cuerpo de Ingenieros de Caminos, Canales y Puertos, Caballero de la Real y distinguida orden de Carlos Tercero, etc.

Certifico: Que como director que he sido de la obras del Puerto de Barcelona, he empleado para la confeccion de los sillares artificiales de hormigon hidraulico de muelle de la muralla de mar, la cal hidraulica de Teil del establecimiento de MM. L. et E. Pavin de Lafarge cuyo material ha correspondido perfectamente al objeto a que se destino, dando resultados sumamente satisfactorios.

Y para que conste asi donde convenga, espido este documento a peticion del interesado, en Barcelona a quince de noviembre de mil ochocientos sesenta y seis.

(Signed) José Rafo.

Barcelone 15*th Nov.*, 1866.

2. Don Mauricio Garrau, Comendador de la Real distinguida orden de Isabel la Catolica, Ingeniero jefe del cuerpo de caminos, canales y puertos. Jefe de la provincia de Barcelona, etc.

Certifico: que se ha marcado con el sello de la oficina de obras publicas de esta provincia, una muestra de hormigon, cortada de uno de los bloques construidos por los SS. Delsol y Martin para las obras del puerto de Barcelona, que se hallan baso me direccion, y cuyo bloque fué construido el dia 6 de octubre de 1863 y sumergido en el mar en abril de 1864, en donde ha permanecido hasta el presente.

El hormigon, que le constituye, esta compuesto en volumenes iguales: de una parte de cal hidraulica de Teil y dos de arena de mar para formar la mezcla o mortero hidraulico; y tres partes de este con cinco de piedra machacada, para construir el hormigon.

Y para que conste, y a peticion de los SS. Delsol y Martin expido la presente en Barcelona a trece de marzo de mil ochocientos sesenta y siete.

(Signed) Mauricio Garrau.

Port of Algiers. (Mediterranean Sea).

The undersigned, Engineer-in-Chief of the Ponts et Chaussées, certifies that the lime of Teil, derived from the quarries of MM. Pavin de Lafarge, has been employed since 1852 in the hydraulic works of the Port of Algiers.

Mixed with sea-sand, it has been used in the fabrication of mortars for concrete immediately immersed, and for artificial blocks immersed after a previous drying in air of from two to two and a half months, according to the season, and the method of use by sea and by land. The mortars thus made have acquired very great hardness, and to-day they do not show any trace of alteration or decomposition by the shock of the waves or by the chemical action of sea-water.

The Engineer-in-Chief certifies, moreover, that Teil lime has been employed successfully in the works in the sea, and that it is very hydraulic, very active and quick, and very homogeneous.

J. DE SERRY.

ALGIERS, *7th March*, 1867.

Port of Oran. (MEDITERRANEAN SEA.)

I, the undersigned, Engineer-in-Ordinary of the Ponts et Chaussées, in charge of the hydraulic works of the Port of Oran, certify, that the piece of concrete delivered to the firm Pavin de Lafarge du Teil (Ardèche), was taken in February, 1861, from an artificial block of 15 cubic metres, immersed in the jetties of the Port of Oran in 1853, after a sojourn of 13 years in the sea; that the concrete was composed of one part of mortar and two parts of broken stone, and the mortar was composed of 350 kilogrammes of Teil lime, derived from the establishment of Pavin de Lafarge, to one cubic metre of sand.

F. ROBIN.

ORAN, *8th February*, 1867.

(Countersigned.)

The Engineer-in-Chief,

AUCOUR.

Port of Philippeville. (MEDITERRANEAN SEA.)

The undersigned, Engineer of the Ponts et Chaussées, certifies that the fragment of block attached to this certificate was made on the 22d March, 1862, and immersed on the 15th October, 1863, on the interior of the small enclosed basin of the Port of Philippeville.

The beton composing this sample is composed of two volumes of broken stone and one volume of mortar; the mortar itself contains per cubic metre of sand, 370 kilogrammes of Teil lime sold by the firm of Pavin de Lafarge; the lime is delivered at Philippeville, screened in powder, and enclosed in sacks.

Besides its well-known qualities, the lime of MM. Pavin de Lafarge is distinguished by an absolute homogeneity.

Certified by the Engineers in charge of the Works.

For the Engineer-in-Chief, DE LANNOY, Absent,

The Engineer-in-Ordinary,

(Signed) GAY.

CONSTANTINE, 28*th Jan.*, 1867.

Port of Ajaccio. (MEDITERRANEAN SEA, CORSICA.)

I, the undersigned, Ingénieur Ordinaire des Ponts et Chaussées, certify that the blocks of concrete numbered consecutively from 1 to 10, are derived from the end of the Margonojo jetty (Port of Ajaccio), executed in 1861 by myself, under the direction of M. Vogin, Chief-Engineer of the Department.

The concrete consisted of three parts of broken stone and two parts of hydraulic mortar; the mortar consisted of 8 parts of sand to 5 of hydraulic lime from the quarries of Teil (Ardèche), belonging to MM. Pavin de Lafarge.

The blocks in question formed part of the foundation of the jetty; they were taken from about 10 centimetres below the level of the sea.

I certify, moreover, to having employed Teil hydraulic lime (quarries of MM. de Lafarge) in various works in the sea, and I declare that the mortars and concretes manufactured with this lime have until now resisted perfectly and have given excellent results.

(Signed) KOZIAROWICZ.

AJACCIO, 11*th Feb.*, 1867.

Port of Bastia. (MEDITERRANEAN SEA, CORSICA.)

1. The block of concrete which is to figure in the Exhibition of 1867, and which bears a ticket giving the number of the present certificate, was obtained from one of the artificial blocks of the revetment of the ancient jetty of the Mole Génois.

This artificial block, of which the upper surface is 0.60 metre below the level of low tide, was made and submerged in 1852, at which time the works were directed at Ajaccio by M. Hernoux, Engineer-in-Chief, and at Bastia by M. Vogin, then Engineer-in-Ordinary of the Northeast Division, and at present Engineer-in-Chief of the Department. The concrete in question consisted of 2 parts of broken stone and one part of hydraulic mortar; the mortar was composed of 0.90 in volume of sand to 0.62 in volume of lime manufactured at Bastia with Teil limestone. A large number of concrete foundations and artificial blocks of concrete have been made at Bastia with Teil lime from the firm of Pavin de Lafarge. These concretes have until now resisted successfully the action of the sea; the sample to which the present certificate refers was chosen as belonging to one of the oldest blocks; the operations were under the supervision of M. Bonavia, Chief Conductor in the Ponts et Chaussées.

Certified as correct by the undersigned Ingénieur Ordinaire,

(Signed) Doniol.

Bastia, 10*th Jan.*, 1867.

2. I, the undersigned, Ingénieur Ordinaire of the Ponts et Chaussées resident at Bastia (Corsica), certify that the hydraulic lime from the Detroit quarries situated in the Commune of Teil (Ardèche) and worked by MM. Couturier, Soullier & Co., is designated in the specifications of the department for works in the sea simultaneously with the lime derived from the Teil quarries of MM. Pavin de Lafarge. I certify, moreover, that the lime of MM. Couturier, Soullier & Co., is employed actually for the South Quay of the Port of Bastia, where until now it has given good results.

(Signed) Doniol.

Bastia, 7*th March*, 1867.

Countersigned and approved by the undersigned Chief Engineer.

(Signed) Vogin.

Ajaccio, 11*th March*, 1867.

Port of Isle-Rousse. (Mediterranean Sea, Corsica.)

The Mayor of the town of Isle-Rousse, Department of Corsica, certifies that the fragment of a block, sent to-day as a sample by M. Padorami of this town, to the firm of Pavin de Lafarge, at Marseilles, has been detached from a huge block immersed in the sea in 1852 during the construction of the works of this port, consisting of pebbles mixed with sand and hydraulic lime under the superintendence of M. Lacroix, Ingenieur-en-Chef des Ponts et Chaussées, and M. Lesguittier, Ingenieur-Ordinaire. In belief of which he has delivered the present certificate.

The Mayor,
Piccioni.

Isle-Rousse, 9*th Feb.*, 1867.

Port of La Spezia. (Mediterranean Sea. Italy.)

1. *Genio Militare.*

Derezione di Spezia Marina.
Arsenale Militare Marittimo di Spezia.

Il sotto scritto in seguito a richista delli Signori Pavin Lafarge, fabbricanti di calce idraulica del Teil (Ardèche) dichiara che nei diversi lavori idraulici di questo arsenale marittimo venne impiegata al giorno d'oggi una quantita di circa tonnellate 3,000 di detta calce del Teil e che y risultati ottenuti riescirono sempre pienamente soddisfacenti.

Tanto attesta il sotto scritto per la pura verita.

Il Maggiore Generale Direttore,
(Signed) Chiodo.

Spezia, *il* 7 *Febbrajo*, 1867.

2. *Servizio del Genio Militare.*

Arsenale Militare Marittimo di Spezia.

Nei lavori di costruzione di questo arsenale militare Marittimo di Spezia si consumaiono nello spazio di un' anno 4,000 Tonnellate di calce idraulica del Teil (Ardèche) proveniente dalla fabrica dei Signori Pavin de Lafarge et Couturier, Soullier & Co., la quale deide ottimi risultati in ogni genere di costruzione sia quando venne impiegata nella formazione all' as ciutto dei muri dell Darsene in cui dopo pochi giorni venne introdotto l'acqua nel qual lavoro si pote osservare prima una repentina présa si detta calci fuori acqua e poscia una resistenza assoluta al constatto delle acqua, sia quando fu adoperata per la formazione di calcestruzzo versato nel mare e di massi artificiali eseguiti fuori acqua nei quali si verifico dopo poco tempo un solido indurimento resistente a forti pressioni senza cedimento o sgranamento.

Perciò questa Direzione del Genio Militare si crede in obligo di manifestare a codesti Signori Provveditori la sua piena soddisfazione sulla buena qualità ed ottini risultati dati dalla sopradetta calce e sul perfetto confezionamento in cui essa arrivo finora in questo porto.

Il Maggiore Génèrale Direttore,

(Signed) CHIODO.

SPEZZIA, 2 *Aprile*, 1867.

City of Tunis. (MEDITERRANEAN SEA.)

Praises be to the One God.

The general of brigade, Mohammed, chief of the municipality of Tunis, who has affixed his seal to the foot of these presents, certifies at the request of MM. Pavin de Lafarge, manufacturers of hydraulic lime, to having had extracted from cisterns constructed in 1863, with the hydraulic lime of this manufacture, a block of *concrete*, which bears as a stamp the seal of the Consulate General of France at Tunis.

He declares, moreover, that the composition of this *concrete* is 350 kilogrammes of hydraulic lime to each cubic metre of sand. Written the 13th of Choual, 1283.

The Chief of the Municipality of Tunis,

(Signed) KAVA MOHAMMED.

17*th February*, 1867.

City of Odessa. (Black Sea, Russia.)

The Paving Committee of the City of Odessa has given this certificate to MM. Pavin de Lafarge, manufacturers of hydraulic lime in the village of Teil (France), and furnishers of this lime for the granite pavement of Odessa, to certify that the sample of pavement delivered to them was taken out on the 8th inst. from the pavement of the military causeway, put down in 1863. The model is one archine in length, and over one-half an archine in breadth ; it consists of ten stones each of seven inches, and is sealed at the four corners with the seal of the President of the Committee. The present certificate is certified to by the signature of the President of the Committee, the counter signature of the Secretary, and stamped with the same seal as the pavement model.

The President of the Committee, Actually Councillor of State,
(Signed) Andriesski.
The Secretary,
(Signed) Fialkovski [l. s].

Odessa, 23*d* *Feb.*, 1867.

Province of Constantine. (Algeria.)

We, the undersigned, Ingenieur en Chef des Ponts et Chaussées, of the Constantine Division, declare that we have employed the hydraulic lime of Teil, from the kilns of MM. Pavin de Lafarge for a great number of various kinds of works, in fresh water as well as in the sea, on the shores of the Mediterranean, and that we have observed in this lime all the qualities of an eminently hydraulic lime of the first order. Not only have the mortars made with this lime acquired in a short time a very great hardness, but they do not appear to be susceptible to decomposition by the sea-water of the Mediterranean. Employed in air, Teil mortars are susceptible of forming masonry of much greater strength than common masonry, and we have observed that in the bridge of El-Kantara during the trial loads made in 1864, the piers of this bridge, built of limestone and Teil lime, supported during 48 hours without damage a pressure of 18 kilogrammes per square centimetre.

We would add that during great heats, many limes are of difficult use, and the mortars made with them are subject to rapid alteration. Now we have observed that the masonry of the El-Kantara Bridge acquired in a short time very great solidity, although during the execution of the works the solar heat was frequently as high as 50 to 57° C.

(Signed) DE LANNOY.

CONSTANTINE, *27th April,* 1866.

Canal of Forez. (FRANCE, DEPT. OF THE LOIRE.)

The undersigned, Ingenieur Ordinaire des Ponts et Chaussées, certifies that MM. Couturier, Soullier & Co., manufacturers of lime of Teil (Ardèche), have furnished in 1866 two thousand and sixty-three tons (2,063 tons) of screened lime for the first division of the Forez Canal, and that from the experiments daily made in the workshops the Teil lime of the above named manufacturers is as eminently hydraulic as that of the Lafarge Works, which was used at the same time in the same works.

(Signed) FEUESTEIN.

ST. ETIENNE, *30th March,* 1867.

Mont Cenis Tunnel.

The undersigned, Engineer of Bridges and Highways, attached to the Construction of Railroads of the Paris-Lyons-Mediterranean Co., certifies having made frequent use of Teil hydraulic lime (Ardèche) in the works under his direction, and having always obtained excellent results, as well in works under water as in tunnels and other works.

In the St. Michel Section, especially in the Mont Cenis Tunnel (13 miles), this lime was used to the extent of upwards of 5,000 tons, notwithstanding the distance from the kilns, and the increase of cost due to transportation. It rendered services which were highly appreciated in all works which required exceptional hydraulic qualities.

The Engineer of the P. L. M. R. R. Co.,

(Signed) F. MORIS.

CHAMBÉRY, *9th Nov.,* 1872.

Railroads.

1. *Lyons & Mediterranean Railroad.*

I certify that I have frequently used since a long time the hydraulic lime of Teil in the works of all kinds which I have had executed in the south of France, and always with uniform success.

The activity of these limes, their homogeneity, and the uniformity of the results which they give, are admitted without question by all the engineers of the South.

The use of the methods of crushing and screening, first put in practice by M. de Villeneuve, add still more to its qualities, and contribute in placing to-day the lime of Teil at the head of all the hydraulic limes of France.

The Ingenieur-en-Chef des Ponts et Chaussées, Director of the Paris-Mediterranean R. R. Co.,

(Signed) PAULIN TALABOT.

PARIS, 12*th March*, 1855.

2. *Southern Railroad.*

The undersigned, Engineer of the Southern Railroad Co., certifies that the contractors of the Bridges of Pinsaguel, on the Garonne river, and of Saverdun, on the Ariegè river (St. Simon & Foix Railroad), as well as of the Castelnaudary Tunnel (Castelnaudary & Castres Railroad), have employed in the construction of a large portion of these works, the Teil hydraulic lime, derived from the establishment of MM. Couturier.

He certifies moreover that the use of this lime has given excellent results.

(Signed) GUILLAUME.

CASTRES, 28*th July*, 1864.

Countersigned.

The Chief Engineer of the Castres Division,

(Signed) A. ALBY.

CASTRES, 17*th Oct.*, 1864.

3. *Paris-Lyons-Mediterranean Railroad.*

The undersigned, Chief Engineer of the Paris-Lyons-Mediterranean R. R. Co., at Marseilles, certifies that since the 27th Feb., 1855, at which time he gave a certificate stating the good results obtained by him in the use of the hydraulic limes of the establishment of MM. L. and E. Pavin de Lafarge at Teil (Ardèche), he has constantly used the lime of MM. de Lafarge, in the works of the Paris-Lyons-Mediterranean R.R. Co., as well as in the constructions of the Marseilles Docks and Warehouse Co., for the parts of said works most subjected to humidity or strains, and that he has never ceased to obtain perfectly satisfactory results.

(Signed) J. DESPLACES.

MARSEILLES, *7th March,* 1867.

PLATE I.

PORT NAPOLEON
GREAT JETTY
MARSEILLES.

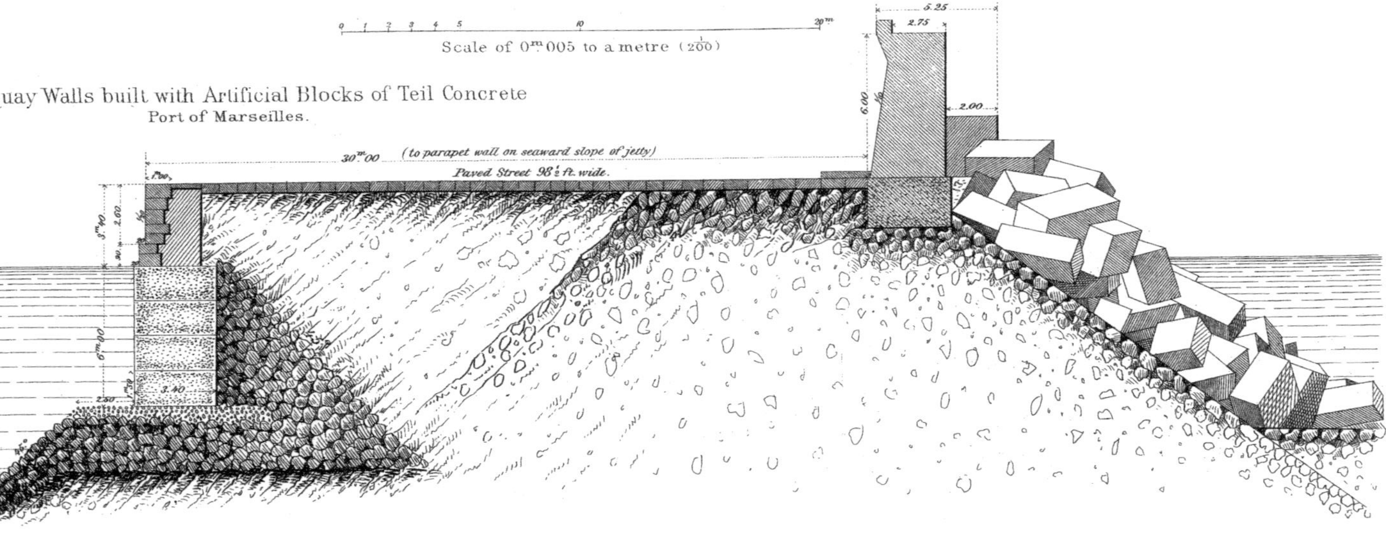

FABRICATION OF MORTAR AND BETON.

SECTION C D.

Scale of $0^{m}.01$ to a metre ($\frac{1}{100}$)

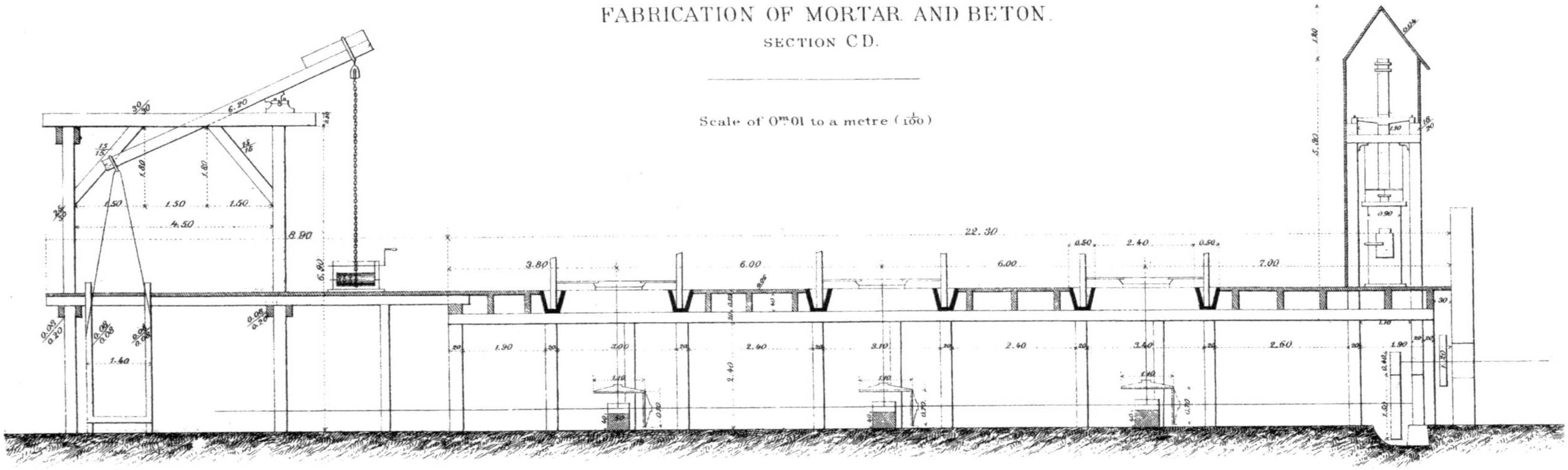

J. Bien, Lith.

FABRICATION OF MORTAR AND BETON

Plan of the upper floor of the Mortar Mills.

Scale: 0^m01 to a metre ($\frac{1}{100}$).

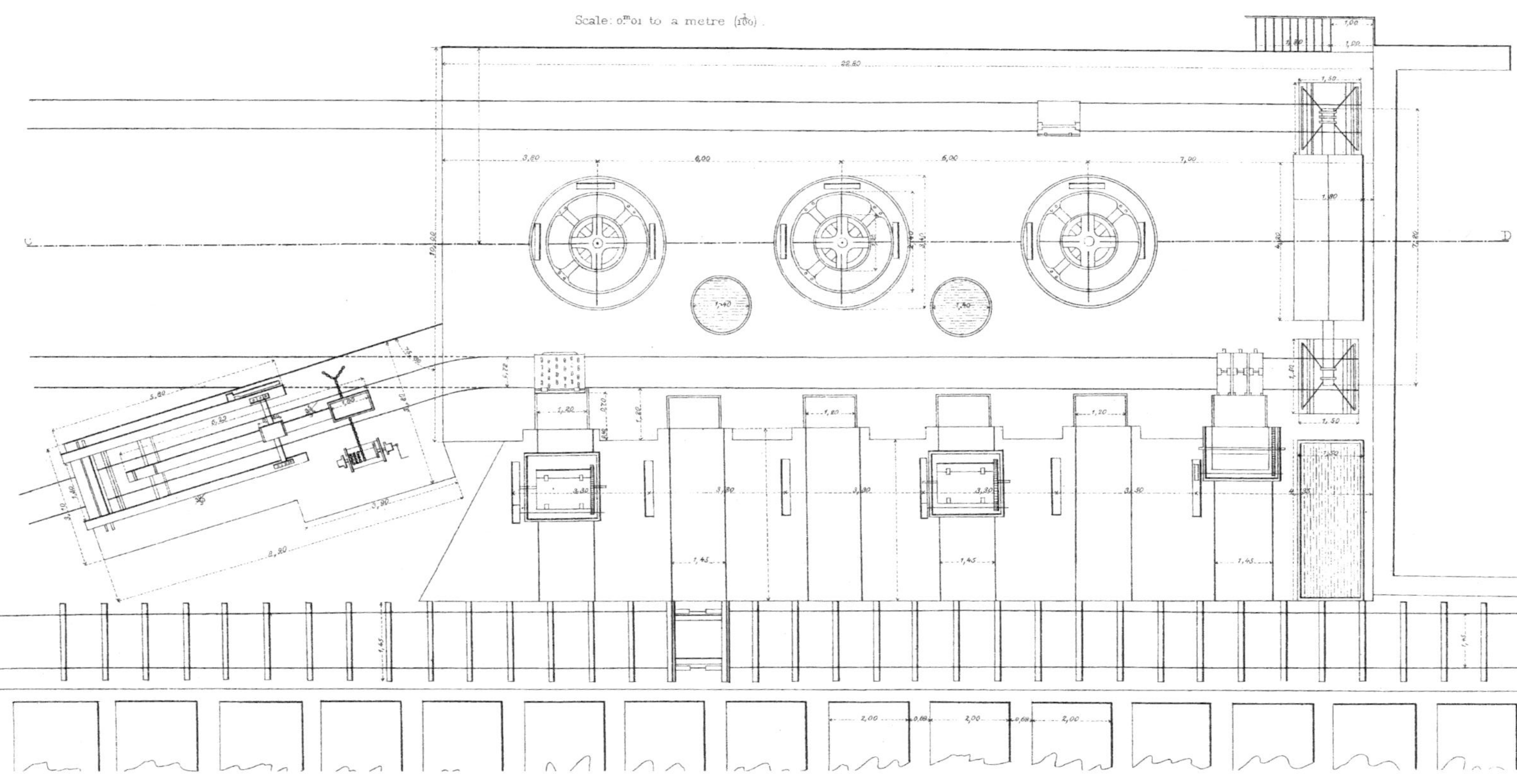

PLATE V.

Sand Car.

Plan

0.20

5

0.30

1.00

5

Section

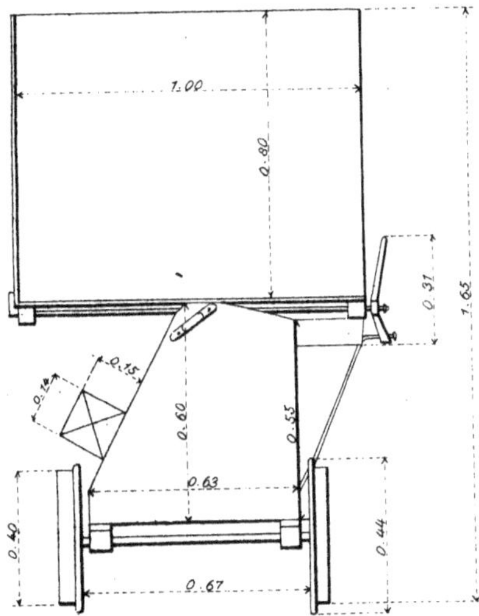

Elevation

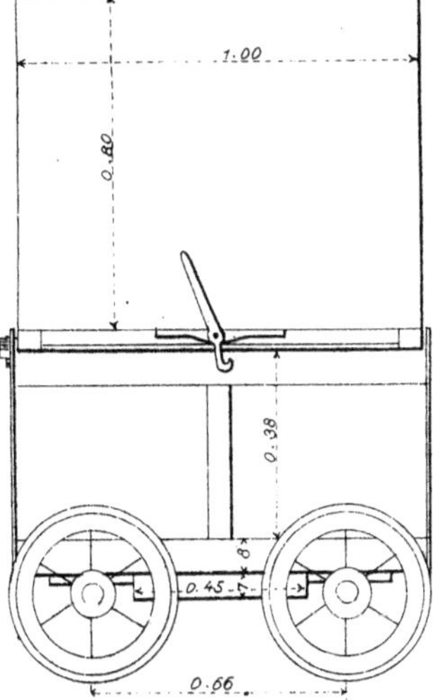

Scale 0m.04 to a metre ($\frac{1}{25}$)

J. Bien, Lith.

PLATE VI

Pebble Car

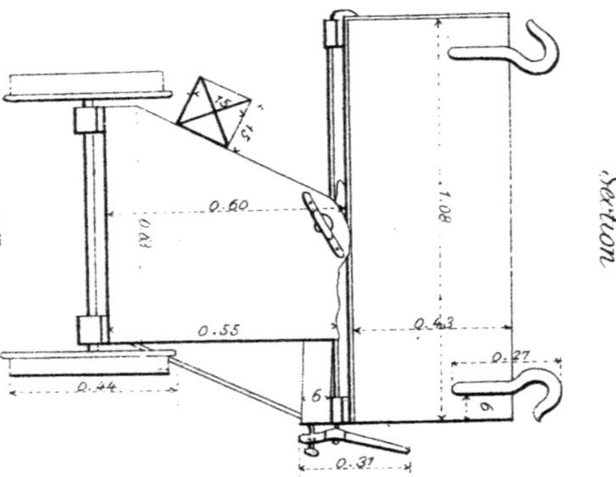

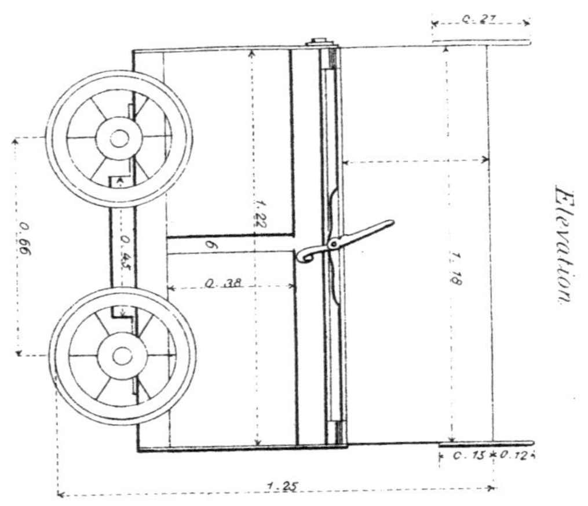

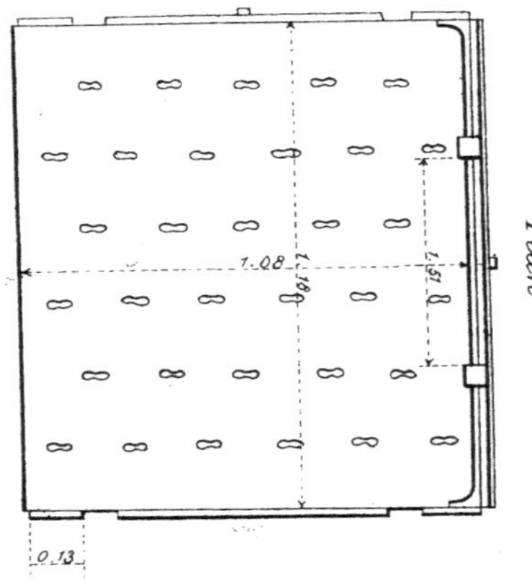

Scale 0.m04 to a metre ($\frac{1}{25}$)

J. Bien, Lith.

PLATE VII

Mortar Car.

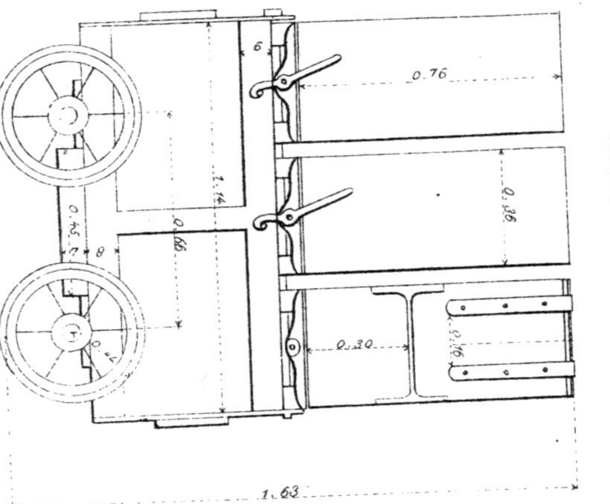

Elevation.

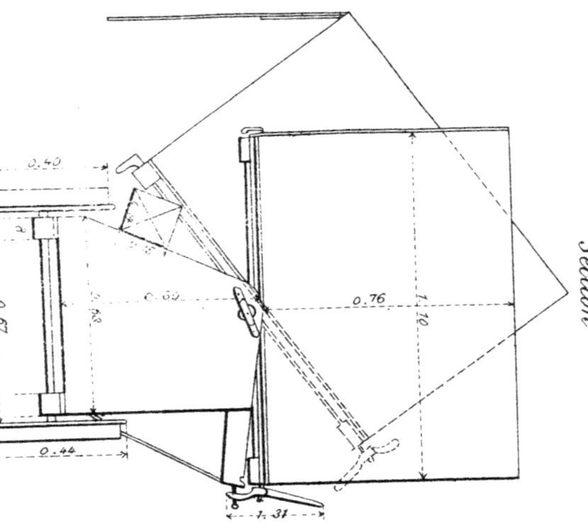

Section

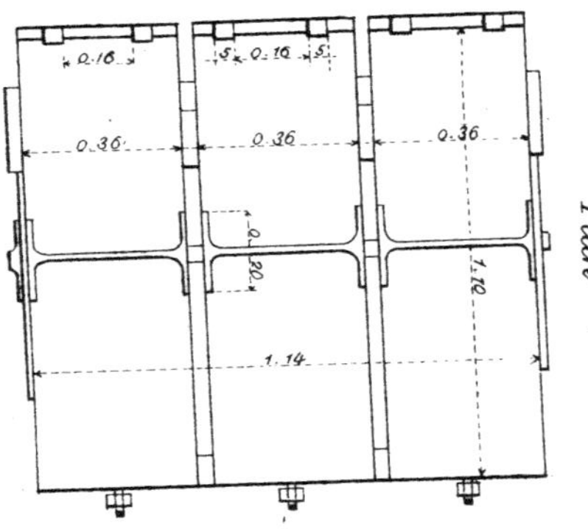

Plan

Scale 0.m04 to a metre ($\frac{1}{25}$)

J. Bien, Lith

PLATE VIII

Mixing Cylinder for Beton.

Scale of 0ᵐ.02 to a metre ($\frac{1}{50}$)

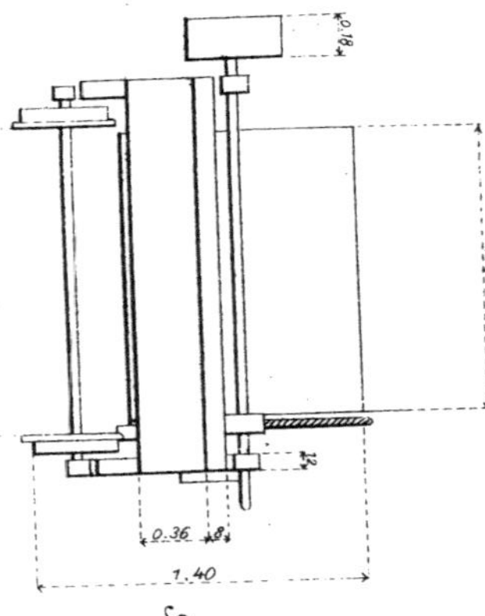

Side Elevation

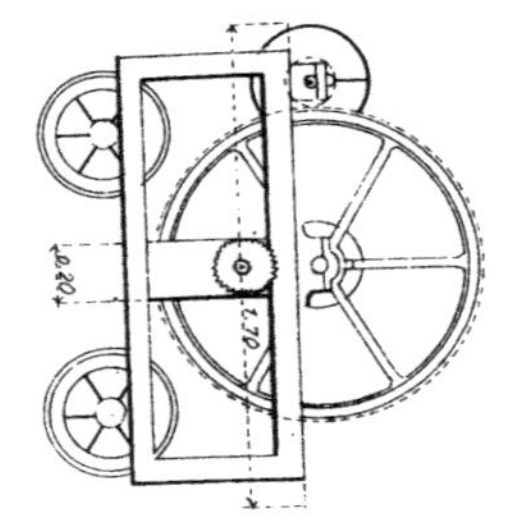

Cross Section

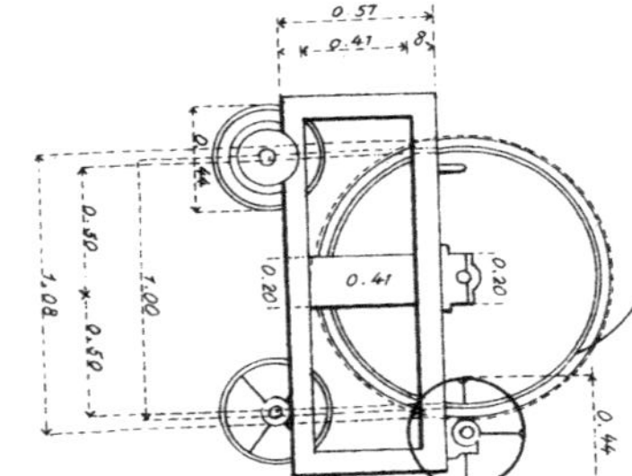

End Elevation

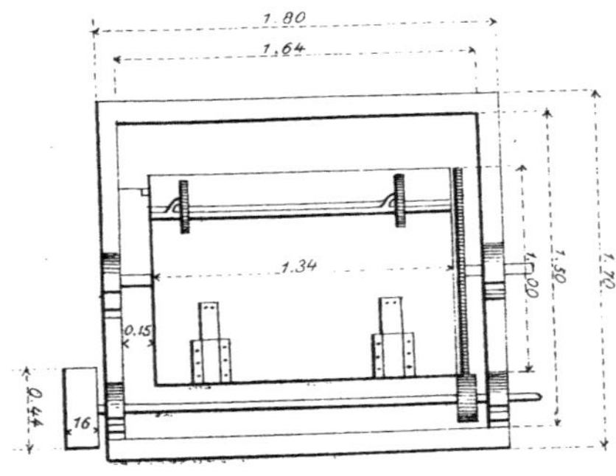

Plan

J Bien, Lith.

Francis' Lowell Hydraulics.

Third Edition.

4to. Cloth. $15.00.

LOWELL HYDRAULIC EXPERIMENTS — being a Selection from Experiments on Hydraulic Motors, on the Flow of Water over Weirs, and in Open Canals of Uniform Rectangular Section, made at Lowell, Mass. By J. B. FRANCIS, Civil Engineer. Third edition, revised and enlarged, including many New Experiments on Gauging Water in Open Canals, and on the Flow through Submerged Orifices and Diverging Tubes. With 23 copperplates, beautifully engraved, and about 100 new pages of text.

The work is divided into parts. PART I., on hydraulic motors, includes ninety-two experiments on an improved Fourneyron Turbine Water-Wheel, of about two hundred horse-power, with rules and tables for the construction of similar motors; thirteen experiments on a model of a centre-vent water-wheel of the most simple design, and thirty-nine experiments on a centre-vent water-wheel of about two hundred and thirty horse-power.

PART II. includes seventy-four experiments made for the purpose of determining the form of the formula for computing the flow of water over weirs; nine experiments on the effect of back-water on the flow over weirs; eighty-eight experiments made for the purpose of determining the formula for computing the flow over weirs of regular or standard forms, with several tables of comparisons of the new formula with the results obtained by former experimenters; five experiments on the flow over a dam in which the crest was of the same form as that built by the Essex Company across the Merrimack River at Lawrence, Massachusetts; twenty-one experiments on the effect of observing the depths of water on a weir at different distances from the weir; an extensive series of experiments made for the purpose of determining rules for gauging streams of water in open canals, with tables for facilitating the same; and one hundred and one experiments on the discharge of water through submerged orifices and diverging tubes, the whole being fully illustrated by twenty-three double plates engraved on copper.

In 1855 the proprietors of the Locks and Canals on Merrimack River consented to the publication of the first edition of this work, which contained a selection of the most important hydraulic experiments made at Lowell up to that time. In this edition the principal hydraulic experiments made there, subsequent to 1855, have been added, including the important series above mentioned, for determining rules for the gauging the flow of water in open canals, and the interesting series on the flow through a submerged Venturi's tube, in which a larger flow was obtained than any we find recorded.

Francis on Cast-Iron Pillars.

8vo. Cloth. $2.00.

ON THE STRENGTH OF CAST-IRON PILLARS, with Tables for the use of Engineers, Architects, and Builders. By JAMES B. FRANCIS, Civil Engineer.

Merrill's Iron Truss Bridges.

Second Edition.

4to. Cloth. $5.00.

IRON TRUSS BRIDGES FOR RAILROADS. The Method of Calculating Strains in Trusses, with a careful comparison of the most prominent Trusses, in reference to economy in combination, etc., etc. By Brevet Colonel WILLIAM E. MERRILL, U.S.A., Major Corps of Engineers. Nine lithographed plates of illustrations.

"The work before us is an attempt to give a basis for sound reform in this feature of railroad engineering, by throwing 'additional light upon the method of calculating the maxima strains that can come upon any part of a bridge truss, and upon the manner of proportioning each part, so that it shall be as strong relatively to its own strains as any other part, and so that the entire bridge may be strong enough to sustain several times as great strains as the greatest that can come upon it in actual use.'"—*Scientific American.*

"The author has presented his views in a clear and intelligent manner, and the ingenuity displayed in coloring the figures so as to present certain facts to the eye forms no inappreciable part of the merits of the work. The reduction of the 'formulæ for obtaining the strength, volume, and weight of a cast-iron pillar under a strain of compression,' will be very acceptable to those who have occasion hereafter to make investigations involving these conditions. As a whole, the work has been well done."—*Railroad Gazette, Chicago.*

Humber's Strains in Girders.

18mo. Cloth. $2.50.

A HANDY BOOK FOR THE CALCULATION OF STRAINS IN GIRDERS and Similar Structures, and their Strength, consisting of Formulæ and Corresponding Diagrams, with numerous details for practical application. By WILLIAM HUMBER. Fully illustrated.

Shreve on Bridges and Roofs.

8vo, 87 wood-cut illustrations. Cloth. $5.00.

A TREATISE ON THE STRENGTH OF BRIDGES AND ROOFS—comprising the determination of Algebraic formulas for Strains in Horizontal, Inclined or Rafter, Triangular, Bowstring, Lenticular and other Trusses, from fixed and moving loads, with practical applications and examples, for the use of Students and Engineers. By SAMUEL H. SHREVE, A.M., Civil Engineer. *Nearly ready.*

The rules for the determination of strains given in this work, in the shape of formulas, are deduced from a few well-known mechanical laws, and are not based upon assumed conditions; the processes are given and applications made of the results, so that it is equally valuable as a text-book for the Student and as a manual for the Practical Engineer. Among the examples are the Greithausen Bridge, the Kuilemberg Bridge, a bridge of the Saltash type, and many other compound trusses, whose strains are calculated by methods which are not only free from the use of the higher mathematics, but are as simple and accurate, and as readily applied, as those which are used in proportioning a Warren Girder or other simple truss.

The Kansas City Bridge.

4to. Cloth. $6.00

WITH AN ACCOUNT OF THE REGIMEN OF THE MISSOURI RIVER, and a description of the Methods used for Founding in that River. By O. CHANUTE, Chief Engineer, and GEORGE MORISON, Assistant Engineer. Illustrated with five lithographic views and twelve plates of plans.

Illustrations.

VIEWS.—View of the Kansas City Bridge, August 2, 1869. Lowering Caisson No. 1 into position. Caisson for Pier No. 4 brought into position. View of Foundation Works, Pier No. 4. Pier No. 1.

PLATES.—I. Map showing location of Bridge. II. Water Record—Cross Section of River—Profile of Crossing—Pontoon Protection. III. Water Deadener—Caisson No. 2—Foundation Works, Pier No. 3. IV. Foundation Works, Pier No. 4. V. Foundation Works, Pier No. 4. VI. Caisson No. 5—Sheet Piling at Pier No. 6—Details of Dredges—Pile Shoe—Beton Box. VII. Masonry—Draw Protection—False Works between Piers 3 and 4. VIII. Floating Derricks. IX. General Elevation—176 feet span. X. 248 feet span. XI. Plans of Draw. XII. Strain Diagrams.

Clarke's Quincy Bridge.

4to. Cloth. $7.50.

DESCRIPTION OF THE IRON RAILWAY Bridge across the Mississippi River at Quincy, Illinois. By THOMAS CURTIS CLARKE, Chief Engineer. Illustrated with twenty-one lithographed plans.

Illustrations.

PLATES.—General Plan of Mississippi River at Quincy, showing location of Bridge. II*a*. General Sections of Mississippi River at Quincy, showing location of Bridge. II*b*. General Sections of Mississippi River at Quincy, showing location of Bridge. III. General Sections of Mississippi River at Quincy, showing location of Bridge. IV. Plans of Masonry. V. Diagram of Spans, showing the Dimensions, Arrangement of Panels, etc. VI. Two hundred and fifty feet span, and details. VII. Three hundred and sixty feet Pivot Draw. VIII. Details of three hundred and sixty feet Draw. IX. Ice-Breakers, Foundations of Piers and Abutments, Water Table, and Curve of Deflections. X. Foundations of Pier 2, in Process of Construction. XI. Foundations of Pier 3, and its Protection. XII. Foundations of Pier 3, in Process of Construction, and Steam Dredge. XIII. Foundations of Piers 5 to 18, in Process of Construction. XIV. False Works, showing Process of Handling and Setting Stone. XV. False Works for Raising Iron Work of Superstructure. XVI. Steam Dredge used in Foundations 9 to 18. XVII. Single Bucket Dredge used in Foundations of Bay Piers. XVIII. Saws used for Cutting Piles under water. XIX. Sand Pump and Concrete Box. XX Masonry Travelling Crane.

Whipple on Bridge Building.

8vo, Illustrated. Cloth. $4.00.

AN ELEMENTARY AND PRACTICAL TREATISE ON BRIDGE BUILDING. An enlarged and improved edition of the Author's original work. By S. WHIPPLE, C. E., Inventor of the Whipple Bridges, &c.

The design has been to develop from Fundamental Principles a system easy of comprehension, and such as to enable the attentive reader and student to judge understandingly for himself, as to the relative merits of different plans and combinations, and to adopt for use such as may be most suitable for the cases he may have to deal with.

It is hoped the work may prove an appropriate Text-Book upon the subject treated of, for the Engineering Student, and a useful manual for the Practicing Engineer and Bridge Builder.

Stoney on Strains.

New and Revised Edition, with numerous illustrations.

8vo. In press. $15.00.

THE THEORY OF STRAINS IN GIRDERS and Similar Structures, with Observations on the Application of Theory to Practice, and Tables of Strength and other Properties of Materials. By BINDEN B. STONEY, B. A.

Roebling's Bridges.

Imperial folio. Cloth. $25.00.

LONG AND SHORT SPAN RAILWAY BRIDGES. By JOHN A. ROEBLING, C. E. Illustrated with large copperplate engravings of plans and views.

List of Plates

1. Parabolic Truss Railway Bridge. 2, 3, 4, 5, 6. Details of Parabolic Truss, with centre span 500 feet in the clear. 7. Plan and View of a Bridge over the Mississippi River, at St. Louis, for railway and common travel. 8, 9, 10, 11, 12. Details and View of St. Louis Bridge. 13. Railroad Bridge over the Ohio.

Diedrichs' Theory of Strains.

8vo. Cloth. $5.00.

A Compendium for the Calculation and Construction of Bridges, Roofs, and Cranes, with the Application of Trigonometrical Notes. Containing the most comprehensive information in regard to the Resulting Strains for a permanent — *t* Load, as also for a combined (Permanent and Rolling) Load. In two sections, adapted to the requirements of the present time. By JOHN DIEDRICHS. Illustrated by numerous plates and diagrams.

"The want of a compact, universal and popular treatise on the Construction of Roofs and Bridges—especially one treating of the influence of a variable load—and the unsatisfactory essays of different authors on the subject, induced me to prepare this work."

Whilden's Strength of Materials.

12mo. Cloth. $2.00.

ON THE STRENGTH OF MATERIALS used in Engineering Construction. By J. K. Whilden.

Campin on Iron Roofs.

Large 8vo. Cloth. $3.00.

ON THE CONSTRUCTION OF IRON ROOFS. A Theoretical and Practical Treatise. By Francis Campin. With wood-cuts and plates of Roofs lately executed.

"The mathematical formulas are of an elementary kind, and the process admits of an easy extension so as to embrace the prominent varieties of iron truss bridges. The treatise, though of a practical scientific character, may be easily mastered by any one familiar with elementary mechanics and plane trigonometry."

Holley's Railway Practice.

1 vol. folio. Cloth. $12.00.

AMERICAN AND EUROPEAN RAILWAY PRACTICE, in the Economical Generation of Steam, including the materials and construction of Coal-burning Boilers, Combustion, the Variable Blast, Vaporization, Circulation, Super-heating, Supplying and Heating Feed-water, &c., and the adaptation of Wood and Coke-burning Engines to Coal-burning; and in Permanent Way, including Road-bed, Sleepers, Rails, Joint Fastenings, Street Railways, &c., &c. By Alexander L. Holley, B. P. With 77 lithographed plates.

"This is an elaborate treatise by one of our ablest civil engineers, on the construction and use of locomotives, with a few chapters on the building of Railroads. * * * All these subjects are treated by the author, who is a first-class railroad engineer, in both an intelligent and intelligible manner. The facts and ideas are well arranged, and presented in a clear and simple style, accompanied by beautiful engravings, and we presume the work will be regarded as indispensable by all who are interested in a knowledge of the construction of railroads and rolling stock, or the working of locomotives."—*Scientific American.*

Henrici's Skeleton Structures.

8vo. Cloth. $3.00.

SKELETON STRUCTURES, especially in their Application to the building of Steel and Iron Bridges. By OLAUS HENRICI. With folding plates and diagrams.

By presenting these general examinations on Skeleton Structures, with particular application for Suspended Bridges, to Engineers, I venture to express the hope that they will receive these theoretical results with some confidence, even although an opportunity is wanting to compare them with practical results. O. H.

Useful Information for Railway Men.

Pocket form. Morocco, gilt, $2.00.

Compiled by W. G. HAMILTON, Engineer. Third edition, revised and enlarged. 570 pages.

"It embodies many valuable formulæ and recipes useful for railway men, and, indeed, for almost every class of persons in the world. The 'information' comprises some valuable formulæ and rules for the construction of boilers and engines, masonry, properties of steel and iron, and the strength of materials generally."—*Railroad Gazette, Chicago.*

Brooklyn Water Works.

1 vol. folio. Cloth. $20.00.

A DESCRIPTIVE ACCOUNT OF THE CONSTRUCTION OF THE WORKS, and also Reports on the Brooklyn, Hartford, Belleville, and Cambridge Pumping Engines. Prepared and printed by order of the Board of Water Commissioners. With 59 illustrations.

CONTENTS.—Supply Ponds—The Conduit—Ridgewood Engine House and Pump Well—Ridgewood Engines—Force Mains—Ridgewood Reservoir—Pipe Distribution—Mount Prospect Reservoir—Mount Prospect Engine House and Engine—Drainage Grounds—Sewerage Works—Appendix.

Kirkwood on Filtration.

4to. Cloth. $15.00.

REPORT ON THE FILTRATION OF RIVER WATERS, for the Supply of Cities, as practised in Europe, made to the Board of Water Commissioners of the City of St. Louis. By JAMES P. KIRKWOOD. Illustrated by 30 double-plate engravings.

CONTENTS.—Report on Filtration—London Works, General—Chelsea Water Works and Filters—Lambeth Water Works and Filters—Southwark and Vauxhall Water Works and Filters—Grand Junction Water Works and Filters—West Middlesex Water Works and Filters—New River Water Works and Filters—East London Water Works and Filters—Leicester Water Works and Filters—York Water Works and Filters—Liverpool Water Works and Filters—Edinburgh Water Works and Filters—Dublin Water Works and Filters—Perth Water Works and Filtering Gallery—Berlin Water Works and Filters—Hamburg Water Works and Reservoirs—Altona Water Works and Filters—Tours Water Works and Filtering Canal—Angers Water Works and Filtering Galleries—Nantes Water Works and Filters—Lyons Water Works and Filtering Galleries—Toulouse Water Works and Filtering Galleries—Marseilles Water Works and Filters—Genoa Water Works and Filtering Galleries—Leghorn Water Works and Cisterns—Wakefield Water Works and Filters—Appendix.

Tunner on Roll-Turning.

1 vol. 8vo. and 1 vol. plates. $10.00.

A TREATISE ON ROLL-TURNING FOR THE MANUFACTURE OF IRON. By PETER TUNNER. Translated and adapted. By JOHN B. PEARSE, of the Pennsylvania Steel Works. With numerous wood-cuts, 8vo., together with a folio atlas of 10 lithographed plates of Rolls, Measurements, &c.

"We commend this book as a clear, elaborate, and practical treatise upon the department of iron manufacturing operations to which it is devoted. The writer states in his preface, that for twenty-five years he has felt the necessity of such a work, and has evidently brought to its preparation the fruits of experience, a painstaking regard for accuracy of statement, and a desire to furnish information in a style readily understood. The book should be in the hands of every one interested, either in the general practice of mechanical engineering, or the special branch of manufacturing operations to which the work relates.' —*American Artisan.*

Glynn on the Power of Water.

12mo. Cloth. $1.00.

A TREATISE ON THE POWER OF WATER, as applied to drive Flour Mills, and to give motion to Turbines and other Hydrostatic Engines. By JOSEPH GLYNN, F.R. S. Third edition, revised and enlarged, with numerous illustrations.

Hewson on Embankments.

8vo. Cloth. $2.00.

PRINCIPLES AND PRACTICE OF EMBANKING LANDS from River Floods, as applied to the Levees of the Mississippi. By WILLIAM HEWSON, Civil Engineer.

" This is a valuable treatise on the principles and practice of embanking lands from river floods, as applied to the Levees of the Mississippi, by a highly intelligent and experienced engineer. The author says it is a first attempt to reduce to order and to rule the design, execution, and measurement of the Levees of the Mississippi. It is a most useful and needed contribution to scientific literature.—*Philadelphia Evening Journal.*

Grüner on Steel.

8vo. Cloth. $3.50.

THE MANUFACTURE OF STEEL. By M. L. GRUNER, translated from the French. By Lenox Smith, A. M., E. M., with an appendix on the Bessemer Process in the United States, by the translator. Illustrated by lithographed drawings and wood-cuts.

" The purpose of the work is to present a careful, elaborate, and at the same time practical examination into the physical properties of steel, as well as a description of the new processes and mechanical appliances for its manufacture. The information which it contains, gathered from many trustworthy sources, will be found of much value to the American steel manufacturer, who may thus acquaint himself with the results of careful and elaborate experiments in other countries, and better prepare himself for successful competition in this important industry with foreign makers. The fact that this volume is from the pen of one of the ablest metallurgists of the present day, cannot fail, we think, to secure for it a favorable consideration.—*Iron Age.*

Bauerman on Iron.

12mo. Cloth. $2.00.

TREATISE ON THE METALLURGY OF IRON. Containing outlines of the History of Iron Manufacture, methods of Essay, and analysis of Iron Ores, processes of manufacture of Iron and Steel, etc., etc. By H. BAUERMAN. First American edition. Revised and enlarged, with an appendix on the Martin Process for making Steel, from the report of Abram S. Hewitt. Illustrated with numerous wood engravings.

"This is an important addition to the stock of technical works published in this country. It embodies the latest facts, discoveries, and processes connected with the manufacture of iron and steel, and should be in the hands of every person interested in the subject, as well as in all technical and scientific libraries."—*Scientific American.*

Auchincloss on the Slide Valve.

8vo. Cloth. $3.00.

APPLICATION OF THE SLIDE VALVE and Link Motion to Stationary, Portable, Locomotive and Marine Engines, with new and simple methods for proportioning the parts. By WILLIAM S. AUCHINCLOSS, Civil and Mechanical Engineer. Designed as a hand-book for Mechanical Engineers, Master Mechanics, Draughtsmen and Students of Steam Engineering. All dimensions of the valve are found with the greatest ease by means of a Printed Scale, and proportions of the link determined *without* the assistance of a model. Illustrated by 37 wood-cuts and 21 lithographic plates, together with a copperplate engraving of the Travel Scale.

All the matters we have mentioned are treated with a clearness and absence of unnecessary verbiage which renders the work a peculiarly valuable one. The Travel Scale only requires to be known to be appreciated. Mr. A. writes so ably on his subject, we wish he had written more. *London Engineering.*

We have never opened a work relating to steam which seemed to us better calculated to give an intelligent mind a clear understanding of the department it discusses.—*Scientific American.*

Slide Valve by Eccentrics, by Prof. C. W. MacCord.

4to. Illustrated. Cloth, $

A PRACTICAL TREATISE ON THE SLIDE VALVE BY ECCENTRICS, examining by methods, the action of the Eccentric upon the Slide Valve, and explaining the practical processes of laying out the movements, adapting the valve for its various duties in the steam-engine. For the use of Engineers, Draughtsmen, Machinists, and Students of valve motions in general. By C. W. MacCord, A. M., Professor of Mechanical Drawing, Stevens' Institute of Technology, Hoboken, N J.

Stillman's Steam-Engine Indicator.

12mo. Cloth. $1.00.

THE STEAM-ENGINE INDICATOR, and the Improved Manometer Steam and Vacuum Gauges; their utility and application By Paul Stillman. New edition.

Bacon's Steam-Engine Indicator.

12mo. Cloth. $1.00. Mor. $1.50.

A TREATISE ON THE RICHARDS STEAM-ENGINE INDICATOR, with directions for its use. By Charles T. Porter. Revised, with notes and large additions as developed by American Practice, with an Appendix containing useful formulæ and rules for Engineers. By F. W. Bacon, M. E., Member of the American Society of Civil Engineers. Illustrated.

In this work, Mr. Porter's book has been taken as the basis, but Mr. Bacon has adapted it to American Practice, and has conferred a great boon on American Engineers.—*Artisan.*

Bartol on Marine Boilers.

8vo. Cloth. $1.50.

TREATISE ON THE MARINE BOILERS OF THE UNITED STATES. By H. H. Bartol. Illustrated.

Gillmore's Limes and Cements.

Fourth Edition. Revised and Enlargd.

8vo. Cloth. $4.00.

PRACTICAL TREATISE ON LIMES, HYDRAULIC CEMENTS, AND MORTARS. Papers on Practical Engineering, U. S. Engineer Department, No. 9, containing Reports of numerous experiments conducted in New York City, during the years 1858 to 1861, inclusive. By Q. A. GILLMORE, Brig-General U. S. Volunteers, and Major U. S. Corps of Engineers. With numerous illustrations.

"This work contains a record of certain experiments and researches made under the authority of the Engineer Bureau of the War Department from 1858 to 1861, upon the various hydraulic cements of the United States, and the materials for their manufacture. The experiments were carefully made, and are well reported and compiled.'—*Journal Franklin Institute.*

Gillmore's Coignet Beton.

8vo. Cloth. $2.50.

COIGNET BETON AND OTHER ARTIFICIAL STONE. By Q. A. GILLMORE. 9 Plates, Views, etc.

This work describes with considerable minuteness of detail the several kinds of artificial stone in most general use in Europe and now beginning to be introduced in the United States, discusses their properties, relative merits, and cost, and describes the materials of which they are composed. . . . . The subject is one of special and growing interest, and we commend the work, embodying as it does the matured opinions of an experienced engineer and expert.

Williamson's Practical Tables.

4to. Flexible Cloth. $2.50.

PRACTICAL TABLES IN METEOROLOGY AND HYPSOMETRY, in connection with the use of the Barometer. By Col. R. S. WILLIAMSOM, U. S. A.

Williamson on the Barometer.

4to. Cloth. $15.00.

ON THE USE OF THE BAROMETER ON SURVEYS AND RECONNAISSANCES. Part I. Meteorology in its Connection with Hypsometry. Part II. Barometric Hypsometry. By R. S. WILLIAMSON, Bvt. Lieut.-Col. U. S. A., Major Corps of Engineers. With Illustrative Tables and Engravings. Paper No. 15, Professional Papers, Corps of Engineers.

"SAN FRANCISCO, CAL., *Feb.* 27, 1867.

"Gen. A. A. HUMPHREYS, Chief of Engineers, U. S. Army:

"GENERAL,—I have the honor to submit to you, in the following pages, the results of my investigations in meteorology and hypsometry, made with the view of ascertaining how far the barometer can be used as a reliable instrument for determining altitudes on extended lines of survey and reconnaissances. These investigations have occupied the leisure permitted me from my professional duties during the last ten years, and I hope the results will be deemed of sufficient value to have a place assigned them among the printed professional papers of the United States Corps of Engineers.

"Very respectfully, your obedient servant,

"R. S. WILLIAMSON,

"Bvt. Lt.-Col. U. S. A., Major Corps of U. S. Engineers."

Von Cotta's Ore Deposits.

8vo. Cloth. $4.00.

TREATISE ON ORE DEPOSITS. By BERNHARD VON COTTA, Professor of Geology in the Royal School of Mines, Freidberg, Saxony. Translated from the second German edition, by FREDERICK PRIME, Jr., Mining Engineer, and revised by the author, with numerous illustrations.

"Prof. Von Cotta of the Freiberg School of Mines, is the author of the best modern treatise on ore deposits, and we are heartily glad that this admirable work has been translated and published in this country. The translator, Mr. Frederick Prime, Jr., a graduate of Freiberg, has had in his work the great advantage of a revision by the author himself, who declares in a prefatory note that this may be considered as a new edition (the third) of his own book.

"It is a timely and welcome contribution to the literature of mining in this country, and we are grateful to the translator for his enterprise and good judgment in undertaking its preparation; while we recognize with equal cordiality the liberality of the author in granting both permission and assistance."—*Extract from Review in Engineering and Mining Journal.*

Plattner's Blow-Pipe Analysis.

Second edition. Revised. 8vo. Cloth. $7.50.

PLATTNER'S MANUAL OF QUALITATIVE AND QUANTITATIVE ANALYSIS WITH THE BLOW-PIPE. From the last German edition Revised and enlarged. By Prof. TH. RICHTER, of the Royal Saxon Mining Academy. Translated by Prof. H. B. CORNWALL, Assistant in the Columbia School of Mines, New York; assisted by JOHN H. CASWELL. Illustrated with eighty-seven wood-cuts and one Lithographic Plate. 560 pages.

"Plattner's celebrated work has long been recognized as the only complete book on Blow-Pipe Analysis. The fourth German edition, edited by Prof. Richter, fully sustains the reputation which the earlier editions acquired during the lifetime of the author, and it is a source of great satisfaction to us to know that Prof. Richter has co-operated with the translator in issuing the American edition of the work, which is in fact a fifth edition of the original work, being far more complete than the last German edition."—*Silliman's Journal.*

There is nothing so complete to be found in the English language. Plattner's book is not a mere pocket edition ; it is intended as a comprehensive guide to all that is at present known on the blow-pipe, and as such is really indispensable to teachers and advanced pupils.

"Mr. Cornwall's edition is something more than a translation, as it contains many corrections, emendations and additions not to be found in the original. It is a decided improvement on the work in its German dress."—*Journal of Applied Chemistry.*

Egleston's Mineralogy.

8vo. Illustrated with 34 Lithographic Plates. Cloth. $4.50.

LECTURES ON DESCRIPTIVE MINERALOGY, Delivered at the School of Mines, Columbia College. BY PROFESSOR T. EGLESTON.

These lectures are what their title indicates, the lectures on Mineralogy delivered at the School of Mines of Columbia College. They have been printed for the students, in order that more time might be given to the various methods of examining and determining minerals. The second part has only been printed. The first part, comprising crystallography and physical mineralogy, will be printed at some future time.

Pynchon's Chemical Physics.

New Edition. Revised and Enlarged.

Crown 8vo. Cloth. $3.00.

INTRODUCTION TO CHEMICAL PHYSICS, Designed for the Use of Academies, Colleges, and High Schools. Illustrated with numerous engravings, and containing copious experiments with directions for preparing them. By THOMAS RUGGLES PYNCHON, M.A., Professor of Chemistry and the Natural Sciences, Trinity College, Hartford.

Hitherto, no work suitable for general use, treating of all these subjects within the limits of a single volume, could be found; consequently the attention they have received has not been at all proportionate to their importance. It is believed that a book containing so much valuable information within so small a compass, cannot fail to meet with a ready sale among all intelligent persons, while Professional men, Physicians, Medical Students, Photographers, Telegraphers, Engineers, and Artisans generally, will find it specially valuable, if not nearly indispensable, as a book of reference.

"We strongly recommend this able treatise to our readers as the first work ever published on the subject free from perplexing technicalities. In style it is pure, in description graphic, and its typographical appearance is artistic. It is altogether a most excellent work."—*Eclectic Medical Journal.*

"It treats fully of Photography, Telegraphy, Steam Engines, and the various applications of Electricity. In short, it is a carefully prepared volume, abreast with the latest scientific discoveries and inventions."—*Hartford Courant.*

Plympton's Blow-Pipe Analysis.

12mo. Cloth. $2.00.

THE BLOW-PIPE: A System of Instruction in its practical use being a graduated course of Analysis for the use of students, and all those engaged in the Examination of Metallic Combinations. Second edition, with an appendix and a copious index. By GEORGE W. PLYMPTON, of the Polytechnic Institute, Brooklyn.

"This manual probably has no superior in the English language as a textbook for beginners, or as a guide to the student working without a teacher. To the latter many illustrations of the utensils and apparatus required in using the blow-pipe, as well as the fully illustrated description of the blow-pipe flame, will be especially serviceable."—*New York Teacher.*

Ure's Dictionary.

Sixth Edition.

London, 1872.

3 vols. 8vo. Cloth, $25.00. Half Russia, $37.50.

DICTIONARY OF ARTS, MANUFACTURES, AND MINES. By ANDREW URE, M.D. Sixth edition. Edited by ROBERT HUNT, F.R.S., greatly enlarged and rewritten.

Brande and Cox's Dictionary.

New Edition.

London, 1872.

3 vols. 8vo. Cloth, $20.00. Half Morocco, $27.50.

A Dictionary of Science, Literature, and Art. Edited by W. T. BRANDE and Rev. GEO. W. COX. New and enlarged edition.

Watt's Dictionary of Chemistry.

Supplementary Volume.

8vo. Cloth. $9.00.

This volume brings the Record of Chemical Discovery down to the end of the year 1869, including also several additions to, and corrections of, former results which have appeared in 1870 and 1871.

*** Complete Sets of the Work, New and Revised edition, including above supplement. 6 vols. 8vo. Cloth. $62.00.

Rammelsberg's Chemical Analysis.

8vo. Cloth. $2.25.

GUIDE TO A COURSE OF QUANTITATIVE CHEMICAL ANALYSIS, ESPECIALLY OF MINERALS AND FURNACE PRODUCTS. Illustrated by Examples. By C. F. RAMMELSBERG. Translated by J. TOWLER, M.D.

This work has been translated, and is now published expressly for those students in chemistry whose time and other studies in colleges do not permit them to enter upon the more elaborate and expensive treatises of Fresenius and others. It is the condensed labor of a master in chemistry and of a practical analyst.

Eliot and Storer's Qualitative Chemical Analysis.

New Edition, Revised.

12mo. Illustrated. Cloth. $1.50.

A COMPENDIOUS MANUAL OF QUALITATIVE CHEMICAL ANALYSIS. By CHARLES W. ELIOT and FRANK H. STORER. Revised with the Coöperation of the Authors, by WILLIAM RIPLEY NICHOLS, Professor of Chemistry in the Massachusetts Institute of Technology.

"This Manual has great merits as a practical introduction to the science and the art of which it treats. It contains enough of the theory and practice of qualitative analysis, "in the wet way," to bring out all the reasoning involved in the science, and to present clearly to the student the most approved methods of the art. It is specially adapted for exercises and experiments in the laboratory; and yet its classifications and manner of treatment are so systematic and logical throughout, as to adapt it in a high degree to that higher class of students generally who desire an accurate knowledge of the practical methods of arriving at scientific facts."—*Lutheran Observer.*

"We wish every academical class in the land could have the benefit of the fifty exercises of two hours each necessary to master this book. Chemistry would cease to be a mere matter of memory, and become a pleasant experimental and intellectual recreation. We heartily commend this little volume to the notice of those teachers who believe in using the sciences as means of mental discipline."—*College Courant.*

Craig's Decimal System.

Square 32mo. Limp. 50c.

WEIGHTS AND MEASURES. An Account of the Decimal System, with Tables of Conversion for Commercial and Scientific Uses. By B. F. CRAIG, M. D.

"The most lucid, accurate, and useful of all the hand-books on this subject that we have yet seen. It gives forty-seven tables of comparison between the English and French denominations of length, area, capacity, weight, and the Centigrade and Fahrenheit thermometers, with clear instructions how to use them; and to this practical portion, which helps to make the transition as easy as possible, is prefixed a scientific explanation of the errors in the metric system, and how they may be corrected in the laboratory."—*Nation.*

Nugent on Optics.

12mo. Cloth. $2.00

TREATISE ON OPTICS; or, Light and Sight, theoretically and practically treated; with the application to Fine Art and Industrial Pursuits. By E. NUGENT. With one hundred and three illustrations.

"This book is of a practical rather than a theoretical kind, and is designed to afford accurate and complete information to all interested in applications of the science."—*Round Table.*

Barnard's Metric System.

8vo. Brown cloth. $3.00.

THE METRIC SYSTEM OF WEIGHTS AND MEASURES. An Address delivered before the Convocation of the University of the State of New York, at Albany, August, 1871. By FREDERICK A. P. BARNARD, President of Columbia College, New York City. Second edition from the Revised edition printed for the Trustees of Columbia College. Tinted paper.

"It is the best summary of the arguments in favor of the metric weights and measures with which we are acquainted, not only because it contains in small space the leading facts of the case, but because it puts the advocacy of that system on the only tenable grounds, namely, the great convenience of a decimal notation of weight and measure as well as money, the value of international uniformity in the matter, and the fact that this metric system is adopted and in general use by the majority of civilized nations."—*The Nation.*

The Young Mechanic.

Illustrated. 12mo. Cloth. $1.75.

THE YOUNG MECHANIC. Containing directions for the use of all kinds of tools, and for the construction of steam engines and mechanical models, including the Art of Turning in Wood and Metal. By the author of "The Lathe and its Uses," etc From the English edition, with corrections.

Harrison's Mechanic's Tool-Book.

12mo. Cloth. $1.50.

MECHANIC'S TOOL BOOK, with practical rules and suggestions, for the use of Machinists, Iron Workers, and others. By W. B. HARRISON, Associate Editor of the "American Artisan." Illustrated with 44 engravings.

"This work is specially adapted to meet the wants of Machinists and workers in iron generally. It is made up of the work-day experience of an intelligent and ingenious mechanic, who had the faculty of adapting tools to various purposes. The practicability of his plans and suggestions are made apparent even to the unpractised eye by a series of well-executed wood engravings."—*Philadelphia Inquirer.*

Pope's Modern Practice of the Electric Telegraph.

Seventh edition. 8vo. Cloth $2.00.

A Hand-book for Electricians and Operators. By FRANK L. POPE. Seventh edition. Revised and enlarged, and fully illustrated.

Extract from Letter of Prof. Morse.

"I have had time only cursorily to examine its contents, but this examination has resulted in great gratification, especially at the fairness and unprejudiced tone of your whole work.

"Your illustrated diagrams are admirable and beautifully executed.

"I think all your instructions in the use of the telegraph apparatus judicious and correct, and I most cordially wish you success."

Extract from Letter of Prof. G. W. Hough, of the Dudley Observatory.

"There is no other work of this kind in the English language that contains in so small a compass so much practical information in the application of galvanic electricity to telegraphy. It should be in the hands of every one interested in telegraphy, or the use of Batteries for other purposes."

Morse's Telegraphic Apparatus.

Illustrated. 8vo. Cloth. $3.00.

EXAMINATION OF THE TELEGRAPHIC APPARATUS AND THE PROCESSES IN TELEGAPHY. By SAMUEL F. B. MORSE, LL.D., United States Commissioner Paris Universal Exposition, 1867.

Sabine's History of the Telegraph.

12mo. Cloth. $1.25.

HISTORY AND PROGRESS OF THE ELECTRIC TELEGRAPH, with Descriptions of some of the Apparatus. By ROBERT SABINE, C. E. Second edition, with additions.

CONTENTS.—I. Early Observations of Electrical Phenomena. II. Telegraphs by Frictional Electricity. III. Telegraphs by Voltaic Electricity. IV. Telegraphs by Electro-Magnetism and Magneto-Electricity. V. Telegraphs now in use. VI. Overhead Lines. VII. Submarine Telegraph Lines. VIII. Underground Telegraphs. IX. Atmospheric Electricity.

Shaffner's Telegraph Manual.

8vo. Cloth. $6.50.

A COMPLETE HISTORY AND DESCRIPTION OF THE SEMAPHORIC, ELECTRIC, AND MAGNETIC TELEGRAPHS OF EUROPE, ASIA, AFRICA, AND AMERICA, with 625 illustrations. By TAL. P. SHAFFNER, of Kentucky. New edition.

Culley's Hand-Book of Telegraphy.

8vo. Cloth. $5.00.

A HAND-BOOK OF PRACTICAL TELEGRAPHY. By R. S. CULLEY, Engineer to the Electric and International Telegraph Company. Fourth edition, revised and enlarged.

Foster's Submarine Blasting.

4to. Cloth. $3.50.

SUBMARINE BLASTING in Boston Harbor, Massachusetts—Removal of Tower and Corwin Rocks. By JOHN G. FOSTER, Lieutenant-Colonel of Engineers, and Brevet Major-General, U. S. Army. Illustrated with seven plates.

LIST OF PLATES.—1. Sketch of the Narrows, Boston Harbor. 2. Townsend's Submarine Drilling Machine, and Working Vessel attending. 3. Submarine Drilling Machine employed. 4. Details of Drilling Machine employed. 5. Cartridges and Tamping used. 6. Fuses and Insulated Wires used. 7. Portable Friction Battery used.

Barnes' Submarine Warfare.

8vo. Cloth. $5.00.

SUBMARINE WARFARE, DEFENSIVE AND OFFENSIVE. Comprising a full and complete History of the Invention of the Torpedo, its employment in War and results of its use. Descriptions of the various forms of Torpedoes, Submarine Batteries and Torpedo Boats actually used in War. Methods of Ignition by Machinery, Contact Fuzes, and Electricity, and a full account of experiments made to determine the Explosive Force of Gunpowder under Water. Also a discussion of the Offensive Torpedo system, its effect upon Iron-Clad Ship systems, and influence upon Future Naval Wars. By Lieut.-Commander JOHN S. BARNES, U. S. N. With twenty lithographic plates and many wood-cuts.

"A book important to military men, and especially so to engineers and artillerists. It consists of an examination of the various offensive and defensive engines that have been contrived for submarine hostilities, including a discussion of the torpedo system, its effects upon iron-clad ship-systems, and its probable influence upon future naval wars. Plates of a valuable character accompany the treatise, which affords a useful history of the momentous subject it discusses. A great deal of useful information is collected in its pages, especially concerning the inventions of SCHOLL and VERDU, and of JONES' and HUNT'S batteries, as well as of other similar machines, and the use in submarine operations of gun-cotton and nitro-glycerine."—*N. Y. Times.*

Randall's Quartz Operator's Hand-Book.

12mo. Cloth. $2.00.

QUARTZ OPERATOR'S HAND-BOOK. By P. M. RANDALL. New edition, revised and enlarged. Fully illustrated.

The object of this work has been to present a clear and comprehensive exposition of mineral veins, and the means and modes chiefly employed for the mining and working of their ores—more especially those containing gold and silver.

Mitchell's Manual of Assaying.

8vo. Cloth. $10.00.

A MANUAL OF PRACTICAL ASSAYING. By JOHN MITCHELL. Third edition. Edited by WILLIAM CROOKES, F.R.S.

In this edition are incorporated all the late important discoveries in Assaying made in this country and abroad, and special care is devoted to the very important Volumetric and Colorimetric Assays, as well as to the Blow-Pipe Assays.

Benét's Chronoscope.

Second Edition.

Illustrated. 4to. Cloth. $3.00.

ELECTRO-BALLISTIC MACHINES, and the Schultz Chronoscope. By Lieutenant-Colonel S. V. BENÉT, Captain of Ordnance, U. S. Army.

CONTENTS.—1. Ballistic Pendulum. 2. Gun Pendulum. 3. Use of Electricity. 4. Navez' Machine. 5. Vignotti's Machine, with Plates. 6. Benton's Electro-Ballistic Pendulum, with Plates. 7. Leur's Tro-Pendulum Machine 8. Schultz's Chronoscope, with two Plates.

Michaelis' Chronograph.

4to. Illustrated. Cloth. $3.00.

THE LE BOULENGÉ CHRONOGRAPH. With three lithographed folding plates of illustrations. By Brevet Captain O E. MICHAELIS, First Lieutenant Ordnance Corps, U. S. Army.

"The excellent monograph of Captain Michaelis enters minutely into the details of construction and management, and gives tables of the times of flight calculated upon a given fall of the chronometer for all distances. Captain Michaelis has done good service in presenting this work to his brother officers, describing, as it does, an instrument which bids fair to be in constant use in our future ballistic experiments.'—*Army and Navy Journal.*

Silversmith's Hand-Book.

Fourth Edition.

Illustrated. 12mo. Cloth. $3.00.

A PRACTICAL HAND-BOOK FOR MINERS, Metallurgists, and Assayers, comprising the most recent improvements in the disintegration, amalgamation, smelting, and parting of the Precious Ores, with a Comprehensive Digest of the Mining Laws. Greatly augmented, revised, and corrected. By JULIUS SILVERSMITH. Fourth edition. Profusely illustrated. 1 vol. 12mo. Cloth. $3.00.

One of the most important features of this work is that in which the metallurgy of the precious metals is treated of. In it the author has endeavored to embody all the processes for the reduction and manipulation of the precious ores heretofore successfully employed in Germany, England, Mexico, and the United States, together with such as have been more recently invented, and not yet fully tested—all of which are profusely illustrated and easy of comprehension.

Simms' Levelling.

8vo. Cloth. $2.50.

A TREATISE ON THE PRINCIPLES AND PRACTICE OF LEVELLING, showing its application to purposes of Railway Engineering and the Construction of Roads, &c. By FREDERICK W. SIMMS, C. E. From the fifth London edition, revised and corrected, with the addition of Mr. Law's Practical Examples for Setting Out Railway Curves. Illustrated with three lithographic plates and numerous wood-cuts.

"One of the most important text-books for the general surveyor, and there is scarcely a question connected with levelling for which a solution would be sought, but that would be satisfactorily answered by consulting this volume." —*Mining Journal.*

"The text-book on levelling in most of our engineering schools and colleges."—*Engineers.*

"The publishers have rendered a substantial service to the profession, especially to the younger members, by bringing out the present edition of Mr. Simms' useful work."—*Engineering.*

Eads' Naval Defences.

4to. Cloth. $5.00.

SYSTEM OF NAVAL DEFENCES. By JAMES B. EADS, C. E. Report to the Honorable Gideon Welles, Secretary of the Navy, February 22, 1868, with ten illustrations.

Stuart's Naval Dry Docks.

Twenty-four engravings on steel.

Fourth Edition.

4to. Cloth. $6.00.

THE NAVAL DRY DOCKS OF THE UNITED STATES. By CHARLES B. STUART. Engineer in Chief of the United States Navy.

List of Illustrations.

Pumping Engine and Pumps—Plan of Dry Dock and Pump-Well—Sections of Dry Dock—Engine House—Iron Floating Gate—Details of Floating Gate—Iron Turning Gate—Plan of Turning Gate—Culvert Gate—Filling Culvert Gates—Engine Bed—Plate, Pumps, and Culvert—Engine House Roof—Floating Sectional Dock—Details of Section, and Plan of Turn-Tables—Plan of Basin and Marine Railways—Plan of Sliding Frame, and Elevation of Pumps—Hydraulic Cylinder—Plan of Gearing for Pumps and End Floats—Perspective View of Dock, Basin, and Railway—Plan of Basin of Portsmouth Dry Dock—Floating Balance Dock—Elevation of Trusses and the Machinery—Perspective View of Balance Dry Dock

---

Free Hand Drawing.

Profusely Illustrated. 18mo. Cloth. 75 cents.

A GUIDE TO ORNAMENTAL, Figure, and Landscape Drawing. By an Art Student.

CONTENTS.—Materials employed in Drawing, and how to use them—On Lines and how to Draw them—On Shading—Concerning lines and shading, with applications of them to simple elementary subjects—Sketches from Nature.

Minifie's Mechanical Drawing.

Eighth Edition.

Royal 8vo. Cloth. $4.00.

A TEXT-BOOK OF GEOMETRICAL DRAWING for the use of Mechanics and Schools, in which the Definitions and Rules of Geometry are familiarly explained; the Practical Problems are arranged, from the most simple to the more complex, and in their description technicalities are avoided as much as possible. With illustrations for Drawing Plans, Sections, and Elevations of Buildings and Machinery; an Introduction to Isometrical Drawing, and an Essay on Linear Perspective and Shadows. Illustrated with over 200 diagrams engraved on steel. By WM. MINIFIE, Architect. Eighth Edition. With an Appendix on the Theory and Application of Colors.

"It is the best work on Drawing that we have ever seen, and is especially a text-book of Geometrical Drawing for the use of Mechanics and Schools. No young Mechanic, such as a Machinist, Engineer, Cabinet-Maker, Millwright, or Carpenter, should be without it."—*Scientific American.*

"One of the most comprehensive works of the kind ever published, and cannot but possess great value to builders. The style is at once elegant and substantial."—*Pennsylvania Inquirer.*

"Whatever is said is rendered perfectly intelligible by remarkably well-executed diagrams on steel, leaving nothing for mere vague supposition; and the addition of an introduction to isometrical drawing, linear perspective, and the projection of shadows, winding up with a useful index to technical terms." —*Glasgow Mechanics' Journal.*

☞ The British Government has authorized the use of this book in their schools of art at Somerset House, London, and throughout the kingdom.

Minifie's Geometrical Drawing.

New Edition. Enlarged.

12mo. Cloth. $2.00.

GEOMETRICAL DRAWING. Abridged from the octavo edition, for the use of Schools. Illustrated with 48 steel plates. New edition, enlarged.

"It is well adapted as a text-book of drawing to be used in our High Schools and Academies where this useful branch of the fine arts has been hitherto too much neglected."—*Boston Journal.*

Bell on Iron Smelting.

8vo. Cloth. $6.00.

CHEMICAL PHENOMENA OF IRON SMELTING. An experimental and practical examination of the circumstances which determine the capacity of the Blast Furnace, the Temperature of the Air, and the Proper Condition of the Materials to be operated upon. By I. LOWTHIAN BELL.

"The reactions which take place in every foot of the blast-furnace have been investigated, and the nature of every step in the process, from the introduction of the raw material into the furnace to the production of the pig iron, has been carefully ascertained, and recorded so fully that any one in the trade can readily avail themselves of the knowledge acquired; and we have no hesitation in saying that the judicious application of such knowledge will do much to facilitate the introduction of arrangements which will still further economize fuel, and at the same time permit of the quality of the resulting metal being maintained, if not improved. The volume is one which no practical pig iron manufacturer can afford to be without if he be desirous of entering upon that competition which nowadays is essential to progress, and in issuing such a work Mr. Bell has entitled himself to the best thanks of every member of the trade."—*London Mining Journal.*

King's Notes on Steam.

Thirteenth Edition.

8vo. Cloth. $2.00.

LESSONS AND PRACTICAL NOTES ON STEAM, the Steam-Engine, Propellers, &c., &c., for Young Engineers, Students, and others. By the late W. R. KING, U. S. N. Revised by Chief-Engineer J. W. KING, U. S. Navy.

"This is one of the best, because eminently plain and practical treatises on the Steam Engine ever published.'—*Philadelphia Press.*

This is the thirteenth edition of a valuable work of the late W. H. King, U. S. N. It contains lessons and practical notes on Steam and the Steam Engine, Propellers, etc. It is calculated to be of great use to young marine engineers, students, and others. The text is illustrated and explained by numerous diagrams and representations of machinery.—*Boston Daily Advertiser.*

Text-book at the U. S. Naval Academy, Annapolis.

Burgh's Modern Marine Engineering.

One thick 4to vol. Cloth. $25.00. Half morocco. $30.00.

MODERN MARINE ENGINEERING, applied to Paddle and Screw Propulsion. Consisting of 36 Colored Plates, 259 Practical Wood-cut Illustrations, and 403 pages of Descriptive Matter, the whole being an exposition of the present practice of the following firms: Messrs. J. Penn & Sons; Messrs. Maudslay, Sons & Field; Messrs. James Watt & Co.; Messrs. J. & G. Rennie; Messrs. R. Napier & Sons; Messrs. J. & W. Dudgeon; Messrs. Ravenhill & Hodgson; Messrs. Humphreys & Tenant; Mr. J. T. Spencer, and Messrs. Forrester & Co. By N. P. Burgh, Engineer.

Principal Contents.—General Arrangements of Engines, 11 examples—General Arrangement of Boilers, 14 examples — General Arrangement of Superheaters, 11 examples—Details of 'Oscillating Paddle Engines, 34 examples—Condensers for Screw Engines, both Injection and Surface, 20 examples—Details of Screw Engines, 20 examples—Cylinders and Details of Screw Engines, 21 examples—Slide Valves and Details, 7 examples—Slide Valve, Link Motion, 7 examples —Expansion Valves and Gear, 10 examples—Details in General, 30 examples—Screw Propeller and Fittings, 13 examples Engine and Boiler Fittings, 28 examples - In relation to the Principles of the Marine Engine and Boiler, 33 examples.

Notices of the Press.

"Every conceivable detail of the Marine Engine, under all its various forms, is profusely, and we must add, admirably illustrated by a multitude of engravings, selected from the best and most modern practice of the first Marine Engineers of the day. The chapter on Condensers is peculiarly valuable. In one word, there is no other work in existence which will bear a moment's comparison with it as an exponent of the skill, talent and practical experience to which is due the splendid reputation enjoyed by many British Marine Engineers."—*Engineer.*

"This very comprehensive work, which was issued in Monthly parts, has just been completed. It contains large and full drawings and copious descriptions of most of the best examples of Modern Marine Engines, and it is a complete theoretical and practical treatise on the subject of Marine Engineering."—*American Artisan.*

This is the only edition of the above work with the beautifully *colored* plates, and it is out of print in England.

Bourne's Treatise on the Steam Engine.

Ninth Edition.

Illustrated. 4to. Cloth. $15.00.

TREATISE ON THE STEAM ENGINE in its various applications to Mines, Mills, Steam Navigation, Railways, and Agriculture, with the theoretical investigations respecting the Motive Power of Heat and the proper Proportions of Steam Engines. Elaborate Tables of the right dimensions of every part, and Practical Instructions for the Manufacture and Management of every species of Engine in actual use. By JOHN BOURNE, being the ninth edition of "A Treatise on the Steam Engine," by the "Artisan Club." Illustrated by thirty-eight plates and five hundred and forty-six wood-cuts.

As Mr. Bourne's work has the great merit of avoiding unsound and immature views, it may safely be consulted by all who are really desirous of acquiring trustworthy information on the subject of which it treats. During the twenty-two years which have elapsed from the issue of the first edition, the improvements introduced in the construction of the steam engine have been both numerous and important, and of these Mr. Bourne has taken care to point out the more prominent, and to furnish the reader with such information as shall enable him readily to judge of their relative value. This edition has been thoroughly modernized, and made to accord with the opinions and practice of the more successful engineers of the present day. All that the book professes to give is given with ability and evident care. The scientific principles which are permanent are admirably explained, and reference is made to many of the more valuable of the recently introduced engines. To express an opinion of the value and utility of such a work as *The Artisan Club's Treatise on the Steam Engine*, which has passed through eight editions already, would be superfluous; but it may be safely stated that the work is worthy the attentive study of all either engaged in the manufacture of steam engines or interested in economizing the use of steam.—*Mining Journal.*

Isherwood's Engineering Precedents.

Two Vols. in One. 8vo. Cloth. $2.50.

ENGINEERING PRECEDENTS FOR STEAM MACHINERY. Arranged in the most practical and useful manner for Engineers. By B. F. ISHERWOOD, Civil Engineer, U. S. Navy. With illustrations.

Ward's Steam for the Million.

New and Revised Edition.

8vo. Cloth. $1.00.

STEAM FOR THE MILLION. A Popular Treatise on Steam and its Application to the Useful Arts, especially to Navigation. By J. H. WARD, Commander U. S. Navy. New and revised edition.

A most excellent work for the young engineer and general reader. Many facts relating to the management of the boiler and engine are set forth with a simplicity of language and perfection of detail that bring the subject home to the reader.—*American Engineer.*

Walker's Screw Propulsion.

8vo. Cloth. 75 cents.

NOTES ON SCREW PROPULSION, its Rise and History. By Capt. W. H. WALKER, U. S. Navy.

Commander Walker's book contains an immense amount of concise practical data, and every item of information recorded fully proves that the various points bearing upon it have been well considered previously to expressing an opinion.—*London Mining Journal.*

Page's Earth's Crust.

18mo. Cloth. 75 cents.

THE EARTH'S CRUST: a Handy Outline of Geology. By DAVID PAGE.

"Such a work as this was much wanted—a work giving in clear and intelligible outline the leading facts of the science, without amplification or irksome details. It is admirable in arrangement, and clear and easy, and, at the same time, forcible in style. It will lead, we hope, to the introduction of Geology into many schools that have neither time nor room for the study of large treatises."—*The Museum.*

Rogers' Geology of Pennsylvania.

3 Vols. 4to, with Portfolio of Maps. Cloth. $30.00.

THE GEOLOGY OF PENNSYLVANIA. A Government Survey. With a general view of the Geology of the United States, Essays on the Coal Formation and its Fossils, and a description of the Coal Fields of North America and Great Britain. By HENRY DARWIN ROGERS, Late State Geologist of Pennsylvania. Splendidly illustrated with Plates and Engravings in the Text.

It certainly should be in every public library throughout the country, and likewise in the possession of all students of Geology. After the final sale of these copies, the work will, of course, become more valuable.

The work for the last five years has been entirely out of the market, but a few copies that remained in the hands of Prof. Rogers, in Scotland, at the time of his death, are now offered to the public, at a price which is even below what it was originally sold for when first published.

Morfit on Pure Fertilizers.

With 28 Illustrative Plates. 8vo. Cloth. $20.00.

A PRACTICAL TREATISE ON PURE FERTILIZERS, and the Chemical Conversion of Rock Guanos, Marlstones, Coprolites, and the Crude Phosphates of Lime and Alumina Generally, into various Valuable Products. By CAMPBELL MORFIT, M.D., F.C.S.

Sweet's Report on Coal.

8vo. Cloth. $3.00.

SPECIAL REPORT ON COAL; showing its Distribution, Classification, and Cost delivered over different routes to various points in the State of New York, and the principal cities on the Atlantic Coast. By S. H. SWEET. With maps.

Colburn's Gas Works of London.

12mo. Boards. 60 cents.

GAS WORKS OF LONDON. By ZERAH COLBURN.

The Useful Metals and their Alloys; Scoffren, Truran, and others.

Fifth Edition.

8vo. Half calf. $3.75.

THE USEFUL METALS AND THEIR ALLOYS, including MINING VENTILATION, MINING JURISPRUDENCE AND METALLURGIC CHEMISTRY employed in the conversion of IRON, COPPER, TIN, ZINC, ANTIMONY, AND LEAD ORES, with their applications to THE INDUSTRIAL ARTS. By JOHN SCOFFREN, WILLIAM TRURAN, WILLIAM CLAY, ROBERT OXLAND, WILLIAM FAIRBAIRN, W. C. AITKIN, and WILLIAM VOSE PICKETT.

Collins' Useful Alloys.

18mo. Flexible. 75 cents.

THE PRIVATE BOOK OF USEFUL ALLOYS and Memoranda for Goldsmiths, Jewellers, etc. By JAMES E. COLLINS

This little book is compiled from notes made by the Author from the papers of one of the largest and most eminent Manufacturing Goldsmiths and Jewellers in this country, and as the firm is now no longer in existence, and the Author is at present engaged in some other undertaking, he now offers to the public the benefit of his experience, and in so doing he begs to state that all the alloys, etc., given in these pages may be confidently relied on as being thoroughly practicable.

The Memoranda and Receipts throughout this book are also compiled from practice, and will no doubt be found useful to the practical jeweller. —*Shirley, July*, 1871.

Joynson's Metals Used in Construction.

12mo. Cloth. 75 cents.

THE METALS USED IN CONSTRUCTION: Iron, Steel, Bessemer Metal, etc., etc. By FRANCIS HERBERT JOYNSON. Illustrated.

"In the interests of practical science, we are bound to notice this work; and to those who wish further information, we should say, buy it; and the outlay, we honestly believe, will be considered well spent." —*Scientific Review*.

Holley's Ordnance and Armor.

493 Engravings. Half Roan, $10.00. Half Russia, $12.00.

A TREATISE ON ORDNANCE AND ARMOR—Embracing Descriptions, Discussions, and Professional Opinions concerning the MATERIAL, FABRICATION, Requirements, Capabilities, and Endurance of European and American Guns, for Naval, Sea Coast, and Iron-clad Warfare, and their RIFLING, PROJECTILES, and BREECH-LOADING; also, Results of Experiments against Armor, from Official Records, with an Appendix referring to Gun-Cotton, Hooped Guns, etc., etc. By ALEXANDER L. HOLLEY, B. P. 948 pages, 493 Engravings, and 147 Tables of Results, etc.

CONTENTS.

CHAPTER I.—Standard Guns and their Fabrication Described: Section 1. Hooped Guns; Section 2. Solid Wrought Iron Guns; Section 3. Solid Steel Guns; Section 4. Cast-Iron Guns. CHAPTER II.—The Requirements of Guns, Armor: Section 1. The Work to be done; Section 2. Heavy Shot at Low Velocities; Section 3. Small Shot at High Velocities; Section 4. The two Systems Combined; Section 5. Breaching Masonry. CHAPTER III.—The Strains and Structure of Guns: Section 1. Resistance to Elastic Pressure; Section 2. The Effects of Vibration; Section 3. The Effects of Heat. CHAPTER IV.—Cannon Metals and Processes of Fabrication: Section 1. Elasticity and Ductility; Section 2. Cast-Iron; Section 3. Wrought Iron; Section 4. Steel; Section 5. Bronze; Section 6. Other Alloys. CHAPTER V.—Rifling and Projectiles; Standard Forms and Practice Described; Early Experiments; The Centring System; The Compressing System; The Expansion System; Armor Punching Projectiles; Shells for Molten Metal; Competitive Trial of Rifled Guns, 1862; Duty of Rifled Guns: General Uses, Accuracy, Range, Velocity, Strain, Liability of Projectile to Injury; Firing Spherical Shot from Rifled Guns; Material for Armor-Punching Projectiles; Shape of Armor-Punching Projectiles; Capacity and Destructiveness of Shells; Elongated Shot from Smooth Bores; Conclusions; Velocity of Projectiles (Table). CHAPTER VI.—Breech-Loading Advantages and Defects of the System; Rapid Firing and Cooling Guns by Machinery; Standard Breech-Loaders Described. Part Second: Experiments against Armor; Account of Experiments from Official Records in Chronological Order. APPENDIX.—Report on the Application of Gun-Cotton to Warlike Purposes—British Association, 1863; Manufacture and Experiments in England; Guns Hooped with Initial Tension—History; How Guns Burst, by Wiard, Lyman's Accelerating Gun; Endurance of Parrott and Whitworth Guns at Charleston; Hooping old United States Cast-Iron Guns; Endurance and Accuracy of the Armstrong 600-pounder; Competitive Trials with 7-inch Guns.

Peirce's Analytic Mechanics.

4to. Cloth. $10.00.

SYSTEM OF ANALYTIC MECHANICS. Physical and Celestial Mechanics. By BENJAMIN PEIRCE, Perkins Professor of Astronomy and Mathematics in Harvard University, and Consulting Astronomer of the American Ephemeris and Nautical Almanac. Developed in four systems of Analytic Mechanics, Celestial Mechanics, Potential Physics, and Analytic Morphology.

"I have re-examined the memoirs of the great geometers, and have striven to consolidate their latest researches and their most exalted forms of thought into a consistent and uniform treatise. If I have hereby succeeded in opening to the students of my country a readier access to these choice jewels of intellect; if their brilliancy is not impaired in this attempt to reset them; if, in their own constellation, they illustrate each other, and concentrate a stronger light upon the names of their discoverers, and, still more, if any gem which I may have presumed to add is not wholly lustreless in the collection, I shall feel that my work has not been in vain."—*Extract from the Preface.*

Burt's Key to Solar Compass.

Second Edition.

Pocket Book Form. Tuck. $2.50.

KEY TO THE SOLAR COMPASS, and Surveyor's Companion; comprising all the Rules necessary for use in the field; also, Description of the Linear Surveys and Public Land System of the United States, Notes on the Barometer, Suggestions for an outfit for a Survey of four months, etc., etc., etc. By W. A. BURT, U. S. Deputy Surveyor. Second edition.

Chauvenet's Lunar Distances.

8vo. Cloth. $2.00.

NEW METHOD OF CORRECTING LUNAR DISTANCES, and Improved Method of Finding the Error and Rate of a Chronometer, by equal altitudes. By WM. CHAUVENET, LL.D., Chancellor of Washington University of St. Louis.

Jeffers' Nautical Surveying.

Illustrated with 9 Copperplates and 31 Wood-cut Illustrations. 8vo. Cloth. $5.00.

NAUTICAL SURVEYING. By WILLIAM N. JEFFERS, Captain U. S. Navy.

Many books have been written on each of the subjects treated of in the sixteen chapters of this work; and, to obtain a complete knowledge of geodetic surveying requires a profound study of the whole range of mathematical and physical sciences; but a year of preparation should render any intelligent officer competent to conduct a nautical survey.

CONTENTS.—Chapter I. Formulæ and Constants Useful in Surveying II. Distinctive Character of Surveys. III. Hydrographic Surveying under Sail; or, Running Survey. IV. Hydrographic Surveying of Boats; or, Harbor Survey. V. Tides—Definition of Tidal Phenomena—Tidal Observations. VI. Measurement of Bases—Appropriate and Direct. VII. Measurement of the Angles of Triangles—Azimuths—Astronomical Bearings. VIII. Corrections to be Applied to the Observed Angles. IX. Levelling—Difference of Level. X. Computation of the Sides of the Triangulation—The Three-point Problem. XI. Determination of the Geodetic Latitudes, Longitudes, and Azimuths, of Points of a Triangulation. XII. Summary of Subjects treated of in preceding Chapters—Examples of Computation by various Formulæ. XIII. Projection of Charts and Plans. XIV. Astronomical Determination of Latitude and Longitude. XV. Magnetic Observations. XVI. Deep Sea Soundings. XVII. Tables for Ascertaining Distances at Sea, and a full Index.

List of Plates.

Plate I. Diagram Illustrative of the Triangulation. II. Specimen Page of Field Book. III. Running Survey of a Coast. IV. Example of a Running Survey from Belcher. V. Flying Survey of an Island. VI. Survey of a Shoal. VII. Boat Survey of a River. VIII. Three-Point Problem. IX. Triangulation.

Coffin's Navigation.

Fifth Edition.

12mo. Cloth. $3.50.

NAVIGATION AND NAUTICAL ASTRONOMY. Prepared for the use of the U. S. Naval Academy. By J. H. C. COFFIN, Prof. of Astronomy, Navigation and Surveying, with 52 woodcut illustrations.

Clark's Theoretical Navigation.

8vo. Cloth. $3.00.

THEORETICAL NAVIGATION AND NAUTICAL ASTRONOMY. By LEWIS CLARK, Lieut.-Commander, U. S. Navy. Illustrated with 41 Wood-cuts, including the Vernier.

Prepared for Use at the U. S. Naval Academy.

The Plane Table.

Illustrated. 8vo. Cloth. $2.00.

ITS USES IN TOPOGRAPHICAL SURVEYING. From the Papers of the U. S. Coast Survey.

This work gives a description of the Plane Table employed at the U. S. Coast Survey Office, and the manner of using it.

Pook on Shipbuilding.

8vo. Cloth. $5.00.

METHOD OF COMPARING THE LINES AND DRAUGHTING VESSELS PROPELLED BY SAIL OR STEAM, including a Chapter on Laying off on the Mould-Loft Floor. By SAMUEL M. POOK, Naval Constructor. 1 vol., 8vo. With illustrations. Cloth. $5.00.

Brunnow's Spherical Astronomy.

8vo. Cloth. $6.50.

SPHERICAL ASTRONOMY. By F. BRUNNOW, Ph. Dr. Translated by the Author from the Second German edition.

Van Buren's Formulas.

8vo. Cloth. $2.00.

INVESTIGATIONS OF FORMULAS, for the Strength of the Iron Parts of Steam Machinery. By J. D. VAN BUREN, Jr., C. E. Illustrated.

This is an analytical discussion of the formulæ employed by mechanical engineers in determining the rupturing or crippling pressure in the different parts of a machine. The formulæ are founded upon the principle, that the different parts of a machine should be equally strong, and are developed in reference to the ultimate strength of the material in order to leave the choice of a factor of safety to the judgment of the designer.—*Silliman's Journal.*

Joynson on Machine Gearing.

8vo. Cloth. $2.00.

THE MECHANIC'S AND STUDENT'S GUIDE in the Designing and Construction of General Machine Gearing, as Eccentrics, Screws, Toothed Wheels, etc., and the Drawing of Rectilineal and Curved Surfaces; with Practical Rules and Details. Edited by FRANCIS HERBERT JOYNSON. Illustrated with 18 folded plates.

"The aim of this work is to be a guide to mechanics in the designing and construction of general machine-gearing. This design it well fulfils, being plainly and sensibly written, and profusely illustrated."—*Sunday Times.*

Barnard's Report, Paris Exposition, 1867.

Illustrated. 8vo. Cloth. $5.00.

REPORT ON MACHINERY AND PROCESSES ON THE INDUSTRIAL ARTS AND APPARATUS OF THE EXACT SCIENCES. By F. A. P. BARNARD, LL.D.—Paris Universal Exposition, 1867.

"We have in this volume the results of Dr. Barnard's study of the Paris Exposition of 1867, in the form of an official Report of the Government. It is the most exhaustive treatise upon modern inventions that has appeared since the Universal Exhibition of 1851, and we doubt if anything equal to it has appeared this century."—*Journal Applied Chemistry.*

Engineering Facts and Figures.

18mo. Cloth. $2.50 per Volume.

AN ANNUAL REGISTER OF PROGRESS IN MECHANICAL ENGINEERING AND CONSTRUCTION, for the Years 1863-64-65-66-67-68. Fully illustrated. 6 volumes.

Each volume sold separately.

Beckwith's Pottery.

8vo. Cloth. $1.50.

OBSERVATIONS ON THE MATERIALS and Manufacture of Terra-Cotta, Stone-Ware, Fire-Brick, Porcelain and Encaustic Tiles, with Remarks on the Products exhibited at the London International Exhibition, 1871. By ARTHUR BECKWITH, Civil Engineer.

"Everything is noticed in this book which comes under the head of Pottery, from fine porcelain to ordinary brick, and aside from the interest which all take in such manufactures, the work will be of considerable value to followers of the ceramic art."—*Evening Mail.*

Dodd's Dictionary of Manufactures, etc.

12mo. Cloth. $2.00.

DICTIONARY OF MANUFACTURES, MINING, MACHINERY, AND THE INDUSTRIAL ARTS. By GEORGE DODD.

This work, a small book on a great subject, treats, in alphabetical arrangement, of those numerous matters which come generally within the range of manufactures and the productive arts. The raw materials—animal, vegetable, and mineral—whence the manufactured products are derived, are succinctly noticed in connection with the processes which they undergo, but not as subjects of natural history. The operations of the Mine and the Mill, the Foundry and the Forge, the Factory and the Workshop, are passed under review. The principal machines and engines, tools and apparatus, concerned in manufacturing processes, are briefly described. The scale on which our chief branches of national industry are conducted, in regard to values and quantities, is indicated in various ways.

Stuart's Civil and Military Engineering of America.

8vo. Illustrated. Cloth. $5.00.

THE CIVIL AND MILITARY ENGINEERS OF AMERICA. By General Charles B. Stuart, Author of "Naval Dry Docks of the United States," etc., etc. Embellished with nine finely executed portraits on steel of eminent engineers, and illustrated by engravings of some of the most important and original works constructed in America.

Containing sketches of the Life and Works of Major Andrew Ellicott, James Geddes (with Portrait), Benjamin Wright (with Portrait), Canvass White (with Portrait), David Stanhope Bates, Nathan S. Roberts, Gridley Bryant (with Portrait), General Joseph G. Swift, Jesse L. Williams (with Portrait), Colonel William McRee, Samuel H. Kneass, Captain John Childe (with Portrait), Frederick Harbach, Major David Bates Douglas (with Portrait), Jonathan Knight, Benjamin H. Latrobe (with Portrait), Colonel Charles Ellet, Jr. (with Portrait), Samuel Forrer, William Stuart Watson, John A. Roebling.

Alexander's Dictionary of Weights and Measures.

8vo. Cloth. $3.50.

UNIVERSAL DICTIONARY OF WEIGHTS AND MEASURES, Ancient and Modern, reduced to the standards of the United States of America. By J. H. Alexander. New edition. 1 vol.

"As a standard work of reference, this book should be in every library; it is one which we have long wanted, and it will save much trouble and research."—*Scientific American.*

Gouge on Ventilation.

Third Edition Enlarged.

8vo. Cloth. $2.00.

NEW SYSTEM OF VENTILATION, which has been thoroughly tested under the patronage of many distinguished persons. By Henry A. Gouge, with many illustrations.

Saeltzer's Acoustics.

12mo. Cloth. $2.00.

TREATISE ON ACOUSTICS in Connection with Ventilation. With a new theory based on an important discovery, of facilitating clear and intelligible sound in any building. By ALEXANDER SAELTZER.

"A practical and very sound treatise on a subject of great importance to architects, and one to which there has hitherto been entirly too little attention paid. The author's theory is, that, by bestowing proper care upon the point of Acoustics, the requisite ventilation will be obtained, and *vice versa*.—*Brooklyn Union*.

Myer's Manual of Signals.

New Edition. Enlarged.

12mo. 48 Plates full Roan. $5.00.

MANUAL OF SIGNALS, for the Use of Signal Officers in the Field, and for Military and Naval Students, Military Schools, etc. A new edition, enlarged and illustrated. By Brig.-Gen. ALBERT J. MYER, Chief Signal Officer of the Army, Colonel of the Signal Corps during the War of the Rebellion.

Larrabee's Secret Letter and Telegraph Code.

18mo. Cloth. $1.00.

CIPHER AND SECRET LETTER AND TELEGRAPHIC CODE, with Hogg's Improvements. The most perfect secret Code ever invented or discovered. Impossible to read without the Key. Invaluable for Secret, Military, Naval, and Diplomatic Service, as well as for Brokers, Bankers, and Merchants. By C. S. LARRABEE, the original inventor of the scheme.

Hunt's Designs for Central Park Gateways.

4to. Cloth. $5.00.

DESIGNS FOR THE GATEWAYS OF THE SOUTHERN ENTRANCES TO THE CENTRAL PARK. By RICHARD M. HUNT. With a description of the designs.

Pickert and Metcalf's Art of Graining.

1 vol. 4to. Cloth. $10.00.

THE ART OF GRAINING. How Acquired and How Produced, with description of colors and their application. By CHARLES PICKERT and ABRAHAM METCALF. Beautifully illustrated with 42 tinted plates of the various woods used in interior finishing. Tinted paper.

The authors present here the result of long experience in the practice of this decorative art, and feel confident that they hereby offer to their brother artisans a reliable guide to improvement in the practice of graining.

Portrait Gallery of the War.

60 fine Portraits on Steel. Royal 8vo. Cloth. $6.00.

PORTRAIT GALLERY OF THE WAR, CIVIL, MILITARY AND NAVAL. A Biographical Record. Edited by FRANK MOORE.

One Law in Nature.

12mo. Cloth. $1.50.

ONE LAW IN NATURE. By Capt. H. M. LAZELLE, U. S. A. A New Corpuscular Theory, comprehending Unity of Force, Identity of Matter, and its Multiple Atom Constitution, applied to the Physical Affections or Modes of Energy.

West Point Scrap Book.

69 Engravings and Map. 8vo. Extra Cloth. $5.00.

WEST POINT SCRAP BOOK. Being a Collection of LEGENDS, STORIES, SONGS, ETC., of the U. S. Military Academy. By Lieut. O. E. WOOD, U. S. A. Beautifully printed on tinted paper.

"It is the work of several different writers, whose names are withheld from the public, but whose contributions all bear a decided flavor of their origin, preserving the unity of a military education and experience. The volume abounds with personal anecdotes and humorous narratives, seasoned with copious specimens of the students' songs, and presenting a vivid, and doubtless a faithful, exhibition of the peculiar lights and shades of West Point life."—*N. Y. Tribune.*

History of West Point.

Second Edition.

With 36 Illustrations and Maps. 8vo. Extra Cloth. $3.50.

HISTORY OF WEST POINT. Its Military Importance during the American Revolution, and the Origin and Progress of the U. S. Military Academy. By Bvt.-Major E. C. BOYNTON. 416 pages. Printed on tinted paper.

"Aside from its value as an historical record, the volume under notice is an entertaining guide-book to the Military Academy and its surroundings. We have full details of Cadet life from the day of entrance to that of graduation, together with descriptions of the buildings, grounds and monuments. To the multitude of those who have enjoyed at West Point the combined attractions, this book will give, in its descriptive and illustrated portion, especial pleasure."—*New York Evening Post.*

West Point Life.

Oblong 8vo. 21 full-page Illustrations. Cloth. $2.50.

WEST POINT LIFE. A Poem read before the Dialectic Society of the United States Military Academy. Illustrated with Pen and Ink Sketches. By A CADET. To which is added the song "Benny Havens, Oh!"

"Summer visitors at West Point will especially enjoy these illustrations; and the poem itself may be regarded as a description of Cadet life, as seen from the inside, by one who appreciates it."—*N. Y. Journal of Commerce.*

Guide to West Point

and the U. S. Military Academy, with Maps and Engravings. 18mo. Blue Cloth. Flexible Covers. $1.00.

SILVER MINING REGIONS OF COLORADO, with some account of the different Processes now being introduced for working the Gold Ores of that Territory. By J. P. WHITNEY. 12mo. Paper. 25 cents.

COLORADO: SCHEDULE OF ORES contributed by sundry persons to the Paris Universal Exposition of 1867, with some information about the Region and its Resources. By J. P. WHITNEY, Commissioner from the Territory. 8vo. Paper, with Maps. 25 cents.

THE SILVER DISTRICTS OF NEVADA. With Map. 8vo. Paper. 35 cents.

ARIZONA: ITS RESOURCES AND PROSPECTS. By Hon. R. C. McCORMICK, Secretary of the Territory. With Map. 8vo. Paper. 25 cents.

MONTANA AS IT IS. Being a general description of its Resources, both Mineral and Agricultural; including a complete description of the face of the country, its climate, etc. Illustrated with a Map of the Territory, showing the different Roads and the location of the different Mining Districts. To which is appended a complete Dictionary of THE SNAKE LANGUAGE, and also of the famous Chinnook Jargon, with numerous critical and explanatory Notes. By GRANVILLE STUART. 8vo. Paper. $2.00.

RAILWAY GAUGES. A Review of the Theory of Narrow Gauges as applied to Main Trunk Lines of Railway. By SILAS SEYMOUR, Genl. Consulting Engineer. 8vo. Paper. 50 cents.

REPORT made to the President and Executive Board of the Texas Pacific Railroad. By Gen. G. P. BUELL, Chief Engineer. 8vo. Paper. 75 cents.

www.ingramcontent.com/pod-product-compliance
Lightning Source LLC
LaVergne TN
LVHW021414110826
845150LV00007B/1919

* 9 7 8 1 4 2 5 5 1 0 4 4 2 *